A BIBLICAL
POINT OF VIEW ON
HOMOSEXUALITY

KERBY ANDERSON

HARVEST HOUSE PUBLISHERS

EUGENE, OREGON

Cover by Dugan Design Group, Bloomington, Minnesota

Cover Photo © Philip & Karen Smith / Taxi / Getty Images

HOMOSEXUALITY
Copyright © 2008 by Kerby Anderson
Published by Harvest House Publishers
Eugene, Oregon 97402
www.harvesthousepublishers.com

Library of Congress Cataloging-in-Publication Data
Anderson, J. Kerby.
  Homosexuality / J. Kerby Anderson.
    p. cm.
  Includes bibliographical references.
  ISBN-13: 978-0-7369-2118-3
  ISBN-10: 0-7369-2118-4
  Homosexuality—Religious aspects—Christianity. I. Title.
  BR115.H6A53 2007
  261.8'35766—dc22
                                                              2007019260

Printed in the United States of America

08 09 10 11 12 13 14 15 16 / VP-SK / 12 11 10 9 8 7 6 5 4 3 2 1

Contents

HOMOSEXUALITY AND SOCIETY

OVER THE PAST FEW DECADES, homosexuality has moved from the margins of society to the mainstream. Even though some homosexuals have not "come out of the closet," the issue of homosexuality has. And it has also become an issue of public policy and morality. Marches for equal treatment under the law have been followed by court decisions granting rights for everything from gay adoption to gay marriage.

When I was growing up in the San Francisco Bay area, homosexuality was beginning to become an accepted lifestyle. My uncle was a homosexual who lived with a male partner, but most people probably thought they were swinging singles because they often had parties at their homes (in California, then Arizona). They were in the travel business and often took trips to promote travel, so their lifestyle was hardly conducive to settling down and having a family. Few people probably paid them much attention.

But during most of the twentieth century in most of the United States, homosexuality was hardly mainstream. That, however, has changed. How did this change occur?

How did we get here?

An important key to understanding this cultural transformation is found in the book *After the Ball,* written by Marshall Kirk and Hunter Madsen.[1] In this book (and an earlier article written by Marshall Kirk and another author titled "The Overhauling of Straight America"), they lay out the strategies homosexuals can use to change the attitudes of Americans about homosexuality. Frankly, much of what they set forth has already been implemented, so their comments were both a blueprint for the future as well as a commentary on a marketing strategy that has already been in place.

The six points of this strategy are as follows:

1. Talk about gays and gayness as loudly and as often as possible.

2. Portray gays as victims, not aggressive challengers.

3. Give homosexual protectors a "just" cause.

4. Make gays looks good.

5. Make the victimizers look bad.

6. Solicit funds from corporations and foundations.

The successful implementation of these six points are a major reason homosexuality has become mainstream in America. Let's see how this has taken place.

First is the call to talk about gays and gayness as often as possible. Over the past few decades, it has been impossible to escape the public discussion about homosexuality. At least one story appears every day in every major newspaper in the country. There are dozens of television programs that have at least one gay character. Sometimes an entire program is devoted to the topic of homosexuality.

This onslaught of coverage makes homosexuality seem like

merely another lifestyle. The purpose, of course, is to wear down those who have moral or religious objections. In their book, Kirk and Madsen say, "The main thing is talk about gayness until the issue becomes thoroughly tiresome."[2]

I understand this reaction. As a talk show host, I wish our show didn't have to spend so much time talking about homosexuality. But every time there is another court decision or legislative action dealing with gay rights, civil unions, or same-sex marriage, we find it necessary to talk about what took place and what the impact may be. At times I weary of the topic and the conversation, yet I realize that ignoring the issue doesn't serve our concerned listeners, who are probably also weary of the topic as well.

Although the book *After the Ball* calls for lots of discussion about gayness, the authors' goal is not to shock. Gay activists work hard to squelch explicit descriptions of gay sex. Kirk and Madsen wrote this warning: "In the early stages of the campaign to reach straight America, the masses should not be shocked and repelled by premature exposure to homosexual behavior itself. Instead, the imagery of sex should be downplayed and gay rights should be reduced to an abstract social question as much as possible."[3]

Another key tactic advocated to garner acceptance of gays is to use churches to change America's perception of homosexuality. Kirk and Madsen argue,

> While public opinion is one primary source of mainstream values, religious authority is another. When conservative churches condemn gays, there are only two things we can do to confound the homophobias of true believers. First, we can use talk to muddy the moral waters. This means publicizing support for gays by more moderate churches, raising theological objections of our own about conservative interpretations of Biblical teachings, and expositing hatred and inconsistency."[4]

Many liberal churches and denominations have been more than willing to publicly support gay rights and homosexuality. This includes the Episcopal Church USA, United Methodist Church, Evangelical Lutheran Church in America, and the Presbyterian Church USA. These and other denominations have fulfilled their desire to gain allies and muddy the moral waters.

Kirk and Madsen also call for an attack on conservative churches that hold to a biblical perspective toward homosexuality. They wrote,

> We can undermine the moral authority of homophobic churches by portraying them as antiquated backwaters, badly out of step with the times and with the latest findings of psychology. Against the mighty pull of institutional religion, one must set the mightier draw of Science and Public Opinion...Such an unholy alliance has worked well against churches before, on such topics as divorce and abortion.[5]

This strategy has been successful and is one more reason for more widespread acceptance of homosexuality in America.

Kirk and Madsen also call for portraying homosexuals as victims rather than "aggressive challengers." This tactic has been successful because people tend to empathize with the underdog. By portraying homosexuals as victims of prejudice and discrimination, gay activists have been able to win sympathy for the "plight" of homosexuals.

Gay activists have been adept at turning tragedies into opportunities to promote the gay agenda. The assassination of Harvey Milk (a homosexual member of the San Francisco board of supervisors) and the brutal murder of Matthew Shepard (a student at University of Wyoming) are two examples of true tragedies that were used to portray homosexuals as victims.

This strategy also gives homosexual activists a "just cause." Gay activists have sought to enlist the support of nonhomosexual members of society to protect homosexuals. Kirk and Madsen wrote, "A media campaign that casts gays as society's victims and encourages straights to be their protectors must make it easier for those who respond to assert and explain their new perspectives."[6]

Kirk and Madsen also call for a campaign to place in a bad light those who have moral or religious objections to homosexuality. They said, "We intend to make the antigays look so nasty that average Americans will want to disassociate themselves from such types."[7]

Unfortunately, this strategy has been successful simply because there are enough mean and bigoted people in society to reinforce this antigay stereotype. For many years, a man by the name of Fred Phelps has picketed the funerals of homosexuals with signs that say such things as "God hates fags" and "God hates America." Christian groups and denominations have denounced his activities, but he still provides a convenient foil for media coverage of antigay attitudes in America. What is often excluded from any media coverage of Phelps is that he has also picketed military funerals and Christian conferences (including ones where I have spoken)—not just funerals for homosexuals.

Finally, much of this work done by gay activists has been funded by various corporate gifts and financial grants. As we will see later, corporate America has been a significant force in the normalization of homosexuality. This ranges from the granting of domestic partnership rights to providing funding for homosexual diversity programs and activities.

What is the gay agenda?

Trying to define the gay agenda isn't easy because the term is applied to various plans and programs set forth by different groups and organizations. The homosexual movement is multifaceted and cannot be reduced to a simple slogan or even a unified set of principles. Obviously, the gay agenda includes a desire for acceptance of homosexuals and even approval of the homosexual lifestyle along with a set of rights and legal structures that support homosexuality. Each organization has a different but interlocking agenda with other organizations.

The Human Rights Campaign (HRC), based in Washington, DC, was founded in 1980 and is the largest homosexual lobby in the nation. HRC "seeks to improve the lives of GLBT [gay, lesbian, bisexual, transgender] Americans by advocating for equal rights and benefits in the workplace, ensuring families are treated equally under the law and increasing public support among all Americans through innovative advocacy, education and outreach programs."[8] The organization works at the federal and state levels through various lobbying efforts, and also works to mobilize grassroots efforts.

The Gay and Lesbian Alliance Against Defamation (GLAAD) is a media watchdog. GLAAD "is dedicated to promoting and ensuring fair, accurate and inclusive representation of people and events in the media as a means of eliminating homophobia and discrimination based on gender identity and sexual orientation."[9] The organization has been described as one of Hollywood's most powerful entities and has had a successful influence on print media.

The National Gay and Lesbian Task Force (NGLTF) is another national organization that works primarily at the community level. The mission of NGLTF "is to build the political power of the lesbian, gay, bisexual and transgender (LGBT) community from the ground up."[10] They accomplish this by training and organizing activists to advance the gay agenda. They also have a

Policy Institute, which has become the homosexual movement's key think tank and provides research and policy analysis for the gay agenda.

The Lambda Legal Defense and Education Fund is a legal organization that is "committed to achieving full recognition of the civil rights of lesbians, gay men, bisexuals, transgender people and those with HIV through impact litigation, education and public policy work."[11] The organization is involved in legal actions primarily through test cases in order to establish legal precedents that advance the gay agenda.

Two other organizations that focus on the education arena are GLSEN (Gay, Lesbian and Straight Education Network) and PFLAG (Parents, Families and Friends of Lesbians and Gays). These organizations are discussed more fully in the chapter "Homosexuality and the Schools." Their goal is to inform administrators, teachers, parents, and students about homosexuality through school programs and clubs.

Have psychologists redefined homosexuality?

The attempt to normalize homosexual behavior began more than 30 years ago. In 1973, activists were able to convince the American Psychiatric Association to have homosexuality no longer described as a "mental disorder" in the organization's *Diagnostic and Statistical Manual of Mental Disorders* (DSM).

The decision to change the manual was not made on account of scientific evidence. It was due to political pressure from gay organizations and activists. Homosexuality was originally listed as a "sociopathic personality," but was changed in 1968 to that of "sexual deviations." In the late 1960s and early 1970s, gay activists began protesting at the annual APA conventions. In 1970, gay activists grabbed the microphone at an APA convention and said, "Psychiatry is the enemy incarnate. Psychiatry has waged a relentless war of extermination against us. You may take this as a declaration of war against you…we're rejecting you all as our owners."[12]

In 1973, the APA board of trustees voted to change the manual's designation, and the next year the voting members accepted the board's decision. One psychiatrist, who witnessed the APA decision later confirmed that the decision was a political one. He said, "The organization was under political assault by gay activists—some of them members of the APA itself. It was easier for the leadership to switch than fight."[13]

There is an interesting footnote to history about one person responsible for forcing the APA to change its designation. He later came out of the closet and wrote *The Joy of Gay Sex* and *The New Joy of Gay Sex*.[14]

Even though the APA made this decision, a survey taken in the 1990s shows that the psychiatric associations in 34 different countries still define homosexuality to be either a pathological or mental illness or a sexual deviation.[15]

How has the gay agenda been advanced in the corporate world?

There are many ways that the gay agenda has been promoted in the business world. One is through the granting of domestic partnership benefits. Approximately one-third of all Fortune 500 companies now provide such benefits even though many in management are not aware of the potential impact these policies will have on their company or on society at large. These are provided for domestic partners of the opposite sex and the same sex and have been successful for advancing the gay agenda.

Sometimes these benefits are granted because of pressure from local governments. In 1996, the San Francisco board of supervisors passed an ordinance that required all companies that do business with the city and county to offer domestic partnership benefits to their employees. This forced many companies to make these benefits available to their employees because they did not want to lose business in one of the top population markets in the United States.

A second tactic used to advance the gay agenda is to convince companies to adopt a sexual orientation policy. Ostensibly these policies are adopted to deal with alleged discrimination in the workplace. Once such a policy is in place, it provides an important foothold for gay activists to enact more of their agenda.

A third tactic is to use corporate policies to promote homosexual behavior through seminars and diversity training. In many of these programs homosexuality is presented in a positive light while biblical convictions about homosexuality are ridiculed and stigmatized. At the very least, these convictions are relegated to personal opinion.

One book dealing with gay issues in the workplace says, "There are people who believe that homosexual behavior is forbidden in the Bible. This too is a personal belief." While discussing marriage this same book says, "Heterosexual language can be changed. We can say, for instance, partner or significant other rather than spouse. We can say, 'Are you in a relationship?' rather than 'Are you married?'"[16]

Yet another tactic is seeking business sponsorship of gay activities and organizations. Corporate America and major corporate foundations have been urged to become major sponsors of the gay agenda. And gay activists have often been very successful at using the media to criticize corporations and companies that do not support their agenda.

HOMOSEXUALITY AND RELATIONSHIPS

THERE ARE NUMEROUS MYTHS and misconceptions about homosexuality. Even with the increasing prominence of homosexuals in society and the continued advancement of their agenda, many of these myths continue to be propagated in the media and the culture at large.

For example, how many homosexuals are there in society? One of the slogans of the homosexual movement is "We are everywhere." But recent census bureau data would suggest otherwise. More than a quarter of all same-sex households reported are concentrated in five urban areas: New York City, Los Angeles, San Francisco, Washington, DC, and Chicago.

Other similar questions include, What percentage of the population is homosexual? Does a person *become* homosexual, or are people born with that orientation? What do we know for certain about the homosexual lifestyle? We will look at the answers in this chapter.

Is 10 percent of the population homosexual?

If a social movement can be defined by a single percentage

figure, that is how the homosexual movement has been defined. For years, the media has said that 10 percent of the population is homosexual. The figure has been used to help normalize homosexuality and argue for special programs in schools for the purpose of ministering to the 10 percent of students who are or will be homosexual. Project 10 is just one such program that has been implemented that derives its name from this statistic.

But is the 10 percent figure really accurate? Many studies suggest that it may be substantially inaccurate. The real figure is probably around 1 to 3 percent.

The Alan Guttmacher Institute study released in 1993 the results of what the *New York Times* called "the most thorough" national study on male sexual behavior. The study found that around 2 percent of the men surveyed had engaged in homosexual sex. The study also found that only about 1 percent of the men surveyed considered themselves to be exclusively homosexual.[1]

The University of Chicago published a study in 1990 based upon a nationwide survey. The study found that active male and female homosexuals were, at most, about 1.5 percent of the total sample of people surveyed. Only 0.7 percent reported having a homosexual encounter within the previous year.

The Minnesota Adolescent Health Survey involved over 36,000 public school students in grades 7 through 12. According to the survey, 0.6 percent of the boys and 0.2 percent of the girls identified themselves as homosexual or mostly homosexual. And 0.7 percent of the boys and 0.8 percent of the girls said they were bisexual.

So where did the 10 percent figure come from? The answer is simple: Alfred Kinsey. The Kinsey Report stated that 10 percent of all men between ages 16 and 55 are "more or less exclusively homosexual" for a three-year period.[2] Notice that Kinsey didn't even say these men were exclusively homosexual throughout adulthood. He estimated that percentage might actually be 4 percent.

Even this percentage is at odds with all the far more recent studies cited above, for good reason. There were serious flaws in Kinsey's research. Whole books have been written about this subject, so let's merely point to one of many flaws in his study. Nearly one-fourth of Kinsey's subjects were prison inmates, with a high percentage of them being sex offenders. One researcher who critiqued Kinsey's findings discovered that Kinsey obtained many of his subjects through a network of contacts that included "male prostitutes, female prostitutes, bootleggers, gamblers, pimps, prison inmates, thieves and hold-up men."³ Also, many who participated in the study were recruited from audiences who had attended lectures on sex in an attempt to find help with their personal sexual problems."⁴

It is simply not true that 10 percent of the population is homosexual. Unfortunately, the slogan used by gay activists still persists, even though solid scientific research has disputed it.

Is homosexuality natural?

Many in the homosexual movement say that their feelings are natural. Often they even say that their feelings are God-given. So how could they be wrong? Years ago a popular song asked how something could be wrong when it felt right. That is the argument from many in the homosexual movement. Their sexual preference feels natural, so it must be natural.

But God's character, as revealed in the Bible, should be our standard. There are many sinful acts that feel natural, but that does not mean they are moral. Romans 1:26-27 makes it very clear that homosexual passions are unnatural:

> For this reason God gave them over to degrading passions; for their women exchanged the natural function for that which is unnatural, and in the same way also

> the men abandoned the natural function of the woman and burned in their desire toward one another, men with men committing indecent acts and receiving in their own persons the due penalty of their error.

Homosexual desires and temptations may feel natural to some people, but they are not what God intends for human beings. Any sexual encounter outside of a heterosexual marriage is immoral. The Bible refers to the sin of sexual immorality nearly four dozen times. Homosexuality, fornication, and adultery are all examples of sexual immorality.

Although God created a perfect world (Genesis 1–2), it was spoiled by sin. The effects of sin impact us physically, emotionally, and spiritually. Homosexual temptation, like other sexual temptations, is a result of the fall (Genesis 3). When Jesus was confronted by the Pharisees, who were the religious leaders of Israel in His day, He reminded them that God "created them from the beginning made them male and female, and said, 'For this reason a man shall leave his father and mother and be joined to his wife, and the two shall become one flesh'" (Matthew 19:4-5). Homosexuality, among other sexual sins mentioned in the Bible, is a perversion of God's plan for humanity.

Is homosexuality a choice?

Although there is good evidence to suggest that people are not born homosexual, that doesn't mean it is always correct to merely refer to homosexuality as a choice. Yes, homosexuals do make choices about their sexual behavior. But that doesn't mean that one morning a man or woman woke up and decided at that moment to be gay or lesbian. When Christians talk about homosexuality as merely a choice, they deny the complexity of human nature and human sexuality.

We don't choose our sexuality or even our sexual identity the way we choose which clothes we will put on in the morning. To say that homosexuality is merely a choice is to invalidate and even insult people who are dealing with very real emotions and temptations in their lives.

Human sexuality is complex, and there is not a one-size-fits-all explanation that accounts for all human behaviors and attractions. Some of the influences begin before a child is old enough to walk and talk. That may explain why certain homosexuals say they were "born that way," since they cannot remember a time during which they were any different.

Other factors include the home environment, the school environment, early sexual experimentation, and a variety of other influences. Positive influences can lead to a healthy sexual identity, and negative ones may lead to a negative sexual identity. But human beings also have free will. So parents should not blame themselves over what a child might do even when raised in the best home environment.

Peer pressure is another very important influence. Each of us has different gifts, abilities, and personalities. That ultimately affects what we do and whom we associate with.

If a young boy doesn't like sports, he may end up spending more time than usual with girls. He may also become very close to his mom. If he does so, other boys will likely call him a sissy or a mama's boy. Over time the label becomes the boy's identity, and that may cause him to do things that lead to the homosexual lifestyle. That doesn't mean the boy sat down one day and decided he would become a homosexual. But a series of choices begun by peer pressure contributed to that result.

A young boy who is molested by another boy or man may be confused by the experience. But the feelings he has may cause him to act on them again. Soon he may be convinced that he is a homosexual. He didn't start out by thinking he would choose to be a homosexual, but the series of experiences he went through took him to that conclusion.

What do we know about the homosexual lifestyle?

In the next chapter we will consider the differences between heterosexual and homosexual relationships. But before we can understand the differences between the two, we need to have a better understanding of the nature of homosexual relationships.

First, there are higher levels of promiscuity among homosexuals than in the general population. While it is certainly true that sometimes the amount of sexual activity among homosexuals has been exaggerated, even gay activists have admitted that it is more than most Americans would imagine. Marshall Kirk and Hunter Madsen reluctantly say, "Alas, it turns out that, on this point, public myth is supported by fact. There *is* more promiscuity among gays (or at least among gay men) than among straights."[5]

One study that was published in the *New England Journal of Medicine* came from a representative sample of non-HIV-infected male homosexuals who kept diaries. On the average, these gay men had 106 partners per year.[6]

One of the classic studies of homosexuals was done by Alan Bell and Martin Weinberg in the mid-1970s. They found that only 14 percent of gay males, and only 40 percent of lesbians, were living in "monogamous" relationships.[7] And the definition of monogamy in these relationships was much different than the common definition. The range of a "monogamous" relationship for a homosexual often lasts no more than nine months and almost never more than five years.

The Bell and Weinberg study also found that 43 percent of gay men estimated they had had sex with 500 or more partners, while 75 percent estimated they had had 100 or more partners.

A later study by these researchers estimated that only 2 percent of homosexuals could be considered monogamous or even semi-monogamous (having ten or less lifetime partners).[8]

Second, because of this reality, researchers and activists have begun to identify what they term "consensual infidelity." This is best illustrated by the work done by Dutch researchers who were studying the spread of HIV among homosexual males in Amsterdam. The researchers discovered that even in so-called "steady" relationships, the homosexual couples had a significant number of sex partners outside of their steady sex partner.

The lead researcher in the study was Dr. Maria Xiridou of the Amsterdam Municipal Health Service. In the introduction she states:

> Data from the Amsterdam Cohort Study (ACS) among young homosexual men suggest that a substantial proportion of new HIV infections occur within steady partnerships. Despite the intensive campaign promoting safe sex practices among homosexual men in Amsterdam, risk-taking remains at substantial levels, especially among steady partners.[9]

The study surveyed the differences in the spread of HIV infections among casual sexual partners and those who considered themselves to be steady sex partners. The researchers found that homosexuals engaging in casual encounters had an average of 16 to 28 sexual partners each year. But those who were in so-called "steady" relationships had an average of 6 to 10 sex partners each year.

The study also uncovered how dangerous this practice of consensual infidelity is. Those involved in the so-called steady relationships were more likely to contract HIV from a steady partner than from a casual partner due to unsafe sexual practices.

How does this relate to the United States? Homosexual activist Andrew Sullivan says in his book *Virtually Normal* that heterosexuals will have to understand that in the homosexual world "the need for extramarital outlets" is far greater than among heterosexuals. He says, "The truth is, homosexuals are not entirely normal; and to flatten their varied and complicated lives into a single, moralistic model is to miss what is essential and exhilarating about their otherness."[10]

There is good evidence to assume that homosexual couples in the United States behave like the homosexual couples in the Netherlands. Essentially, monogamy and homosexuality are contradictory terms.

Are gay teens committing suicide in alarming numbers?

One of the myths circulating through the homosexual community is that 30 percent of all teen suicides are the result of kids struggling with their homosexuality in a society that shuns them or ridicules them. The origin of this myth came from a paper published in 1989 entitled, "Gay Male and Lesbian Youth Suicide."[11] The study was a bombshell that gained popular attention and also gained significant credibility when it was published in the *Health and Human Services Journal.*

At the time, the Secretary of Health and Human Services denounced the paper as flawed. Dr. Louis Sullivan said that the views in the paper "do not in any way represent my personal beliefs or the policy of this Department."[12] In fact, the paper was full of erroneous information and inferences.

First, the paper assumed that 10 percent of the populace is homosexual. As we have already seen, that figure is grossly exaggerated. So the baseline percentage used for the rest of the report was flawed, thus leading to flawed conclusions.

Second, the report used as a "finding" a statistic that was

published in a 1985 edition of the gay newspaper the *Washington Blade.*[13] An article suggested that 3000 gay youth commit suicide each year. The problem with that statistic was that it exceeded the total number of suicides by all teens in that year!

Third, a later study done by a Cornell University professor disproved the 30 percent statistic. It showed that nearly all the research on this topic was drawn from support groups or shelters where troubled teens gather and was not representative of the population as a whole. This study concluded that gay and lesbian teenagers were only slightly more likely to commit suicide than their nonhomosexual counterparts.[14]

Other significant flaws in the study have been documented in an article in *The Journal of Human Sexuality.*[15] But that has not stopped some in the gay community from using the statistic to argue for homosexual education in the schools and to argue for greater tolerance and acceptance of the gay lifestyle in society.

What are the medical consequences of homosexuality?

During the 1980s, there were many research papers and journal articles about the incidence of HIV infection among male homosexuals. Now that the AIDS scare has died down, most people are unaware that there are many other medical consequences to homosexual behavior.

An article in the *Annals of Internal Medicine* listed over 15 severe injuries, diseases, or syndromes associated with oral and anal sex. These included rectal tearing and hepatitis A and hepatitis B. The article went on to note that the Centers for Disease Control reported almost half of male patients with syphilis claimed homosexual or bisexual contacts, despite the fact that homosexuals constitute only a small percentage of the population.[16]

Other studies have shown that homosexuals account for 80 percent of America's most serious sexually transmitted diseases

(STDs).[17] An article in the *Archives of Internal Medicine* reported that homosexual men contracted syphilis at three to four times the rate of heterosexuals.[18] Another study found that youths who engage in homosexual behavior are 22 times more likely to contract an STD than strictly heterosexual youths.[19]

A study of lesbians found a "relatively high prevalence of the viral STDs, herpes simplex and human papillomavirus." Another study also found bacterial vaginosis occurring in 33 percent of lesbians but only 13 percent of heterosexual women.[20]

The medical impact on life expectancy is predictable. In 1997 researchers at St. Paul's Hospital in Vancouver, British Columbia, published a report in the *International Journal of Epidemiology*. They concluded, "In a major Canadian centre, life expectancy at age 20 years for gay and bisexual men is 8 to 20 years less than for all men. If the same pattern of mortality were to continue, we estimate that nearly half of gay and bisexual men currently 20 years of age will not reach their 65th birthday."[21]

HOMOSEXUALITY AND FAMILIES

FAMILIES ARE THE FOUNDATION OF SOCIETY. When society seeks to redefine marriage and family, what is the impact? What about the important emotional and physical benefits that are derived from traditional families? These questions are being asked by many people today and deserve answers based upon the best social research available.

Similar questions are beginning to surface about the impact of homosexuality on families. Are heterosexual couples and homosexual couples the same or different? Does the fact that a teenager expresses homosexual tendencies always mean that teen is homosexual? What about the issue of adoption by homosexual parents?

What are the benefits of traditional marriage?

Traditional marriages are the foundation of civilization. So before we even consider the impact of homosexuality, same-sex marriage, and other alternative lifestyles, we should consider the benefits of traditional marriage to society.

An excellent summary of the studies done on married people can be found in the book *The Case for Marriage: Why Married*

People are Happier, Healthier, and Better Off Financially by Linda Waite and Maggie Gallagher.[1] Here are just a few of the many findings:

- Married people are much happier and likely to be less unhappy than any other group of people.

- Married people live up to eight years longer than divorced or never-married people.

- Married people suffer less from long-term illnesses than those who are unmarried.

- Married people are less likely to engage in unhealthy behaviors such as drug and alcohol abuse.

- Married people have twice the amount of sex single people have and report greater levels of satisfaction in the area of sexual intimacy.

A look at individual studies by social scientists also confirms these conclusions. For example, married men and women report greater satisfaction with family life.[2] Married couples report greater sexual satisfaction,[3] and married women report higher levels of physical and psychological health.[4] Married people experience less depression.[5]

> "The vast majority of people do better if men marry women. The sexes complement each other. Having a woman in your household makes men better, and having a man in your household makes women better."[6]
>
> **James Q. Wilson**

Researchers at the Heritage Foundation have also compiled numerous statistics that also demonstrate the positive impact of marriage. Traditional marriages have higher incomes when compared to stepfamilies, cohabiting couples, or those who never married.[7] Traditional marriages also result in lower welfare costs to society when compared to divorced couples or out-of-wedlock births.[8] Married women are less likely to be victims of domestic violence, and married men and women are more likely to be happy and less likely to attempt suicide.[9]

The studies compiled by the Heritage Foundation also found many positive effects on children.[10] For example, they found that children in a traditional family are less likely to...

- suffer serious child abuse

- end up in jail as adults

- be depressed as adolescents

- be expelled from school

- repeat a grade in school

- have developmental problems

- have behavioral problems

- use drugs (marijuana, cocaine)

- be sexually active

Children benefit from traditional marriages in the same way adults do. For example, they are better off financially. The National Longitudinal Survey of Youth found that child poverty increased dramatically outside of intact marriages.[11] Children in married homes are generally healthier physically and emotionally when they reach adulthood than children from other home situations.[12]

Although these are relatively recent studies, the conclusions have been known for much longer. In the 1930s, British anthropologist J.D. Unwin studied 86 different cultures stretching across 5,000 years. He found that when a society restricted sex to a traditional marriage, it thrived. He also found that when a society weakened the sexual ethic of marriage, it deteriorated and eventually disintegrated.[13]

Pitirim Sorokin, the founder of sociology at Harvard University, believed that the regulation of sexuality was the first mark of civilization. According to him, civilization is possible only when marriage is normative and sexual urges are restricted. The members of society were often oblivious to their eventual collapse. He wrote,

> Most peoples of decaying societies were unaware of their cancerous sickness. Most of them were sanguine about their present state and future prospects. They continued to live cheerfully in a fool's paradise...they attacked all honest appraisals of the situation, and called them false prophecies of doom and gloom.[14]

Are heterosexual and homosexual couples different?

The popular media treats heterosexual and homosexual couples as if they are no different from one another. One headline proclaimed "Married and Gay Couples Not All that Different" and essentially said they were just like the couple next door.[15]

There is good reason to question that assumption. Dr. Timothy Dailey is among those who have compiled numerous statistics that demonstrate significant differences.[16] He shows that "committed" homosexual relationships are radically different from heterosexual marriage relationships in at least six ways: relationship duration, monogamy versus promiscuity, relationship commitment, number of children being raised, health risks, and rates of intimate partner violence.

Consider the duration of a relationship. Gay activists often point to the high divorce rates among married couples and suggest that heterosexuals fare no better than homosexuals. Research shows, however, that male homosexual relationships last only a fraction of the length of most marriages. By contrast, the National Center for Health Statistics reported that 66 percent of first traditional marriages last ten years or longer, with 50 percent lasting 20 years or longer.[17]

Various studies of homosexual relationships show a much different picture. For example, the Gay/Lesbian Consumer Online Census of nearly 8000 homosexuals found that only 15 percent described their "current relationship" as having lasted 12 years or longer.[18] A study of homosexual men in the Netherlands published in the journal *AIDS* found that the "duration of steady partnerships" was 1.5 years.[19] In a study of male homosexuality in *Western Sexuality: Practice and Precept in Past and Present Times,* Pollak found that "few homosexual relationships last longer than two years, with many men reporting hundreds of lifetime partners."[20]

Another key difference is monogamy versus promiscuity. Married heterosexual couples are more monogamous than the popular culture and media would have you believe. A national survey published in the *Journal of Sex Research* found that 77 percent of married men and 88 percent of married women had remained faithful to their marriage vows.[21] A national survey in *The Social Organization of Sexuality: Sexual Practices in the United States* came to essentially the same conclusions (75 percent of husbands and 85 percent of wives).[22]

By contrast, homosexuals were much less monogamous and much more promiscuous. In the classic study by Bell and Weinberg, these researchers found that 43 percent of white male homosexuals had sex with 500 or more partners, with 28 percent having 1000 or more sex partners.[23] And a Dutch study of partnered homosexuals, published in the journal *AIDS,* found that men with a "steady partner" nevertheless had an average of eight sexual partners per year.[24]

The authors of *The Male Couple* reported in their study of 156 males in homosexual relationships lasting from one to 37 years that "only seven couples have a totally exclusive sexual relationship, and these men all have been together for less than five years. Stated another way, all couples with a relationship lasting more than five years have incorporated some provision for outside sexual activity in their relationships."[25] They also found that most homosexual

---

Point of View: You wrote a book titled *Preventing Homosexuality.* Why would parents want to do that?

Dr. Nicolosi: I am a member of a psychological profession. And they believe that there is nothing wrong with homosexuality and can't imagine why parents would be concerned about the issue. But in the real world, parents are concerned. Given the choice, most parents would rather have their child heterosexual rather than homosexual. This is not homophobia. It is simply the fact that living your life as a heterosexual is much easier than living your life as a homosexual. Being 98 percent of the population is a lot easier than being part of 2 percent of the population.

Point of View: What is the danger of ignoring GID (Gender Identity Disorder) rather than leaving it alone?

Dr. Nicolosi: The general advice of my profession is that if you see the predictors of homosexuality, you should do nothing. It is a political piece of information. It's not a scientific piece of information. And if you do leave them alone, there is a 75 percent predictability of [becoming homosexual, bisexual, or transgender].

—Interview with **Dr. Joseph Nicolosi**
on *Point of View* radio talk show[26]

---

men understood sexual relations outside the relationship to be the norm and usually viewed standards of monogamy as an act of oppression.

A third difference between heterosexual and homosexual couples is level of commitment. Timothy Dailey argues, "If homosexuals and lesbians truly desired the same kind of commitment signified by marriage, then one would expect them to take advantage of the opportunity to enter into civil unions or registered partnerships."[27] This would provide them with legal recognition as well as legal rights. However, it is clear that few homosexuals and lesbians have chosen to take advantage of these various unions (same-sex marriages, civil unions, domestic partnerships). This suggests a difference in commitment level compared to that exhibited by married couples.

These three differences (along with others detailed by Timothy Dailey) demonstrate there are significant differences between heterosexual and homosexual relationships. Gay and lesbian couples are less likely to commit themselves to the type of monogamous relationship found in a traditional marriage.

What about teens and homosexuality?

Teenagers live in a world saturated with sexual messages. These messages not only convince heterosexual teenagers to engage in sex, but some messages also contribute to gender confusion. Add to this the peer pressure and school programs that often push young children to decide early if they are gay, straight, or bisexual. It is a confusing time for young people, and the latest studies confirm this.

For example, a study published in the journal *Pediatrics* determined that by age 12, already one-fourth of the students surveyed were unsure of their sexual orientation. At a time when their bodies were just beginning to go through puberty, essentially they were being asked if they were gay, straight, or bisexual.[28] The study also found that by age 17, only 5 percent of the students were unsure of their sexual orientation.

Teenagers often experiment with many things in their lives: alcohol, drugs, sex. But there is good evidence to suggest that a teenager who experiments with homosexual sex will not remain in that lifestyle. Psychiatrist Dr. Jeffrey Satinover cites statistics from the National Health and Social Life Survey, which is considered the most comprehensive study of sexuality. The study found that about "ten out of every 100 men have had sex with another man at some time—the origin of the 10% gay myth." He adds that "by age twenty-five, the percentage of gay identified men drops to 2.8%." This is his conclusion:

> So what does this mean? It means that without any inter-
> vention whatsoever, three out of four boys who think
> they're gay at age 16 aren't by 25. So if we're going to treat
> homosexuality as a state, 75% of "gays" become "non-
> gay" spontaneously. That's a statement which I consider
> ludicrous, but if you accept this tacit proposition—that
> being gay is an actual state, like being short or being tall,
> black or white—then in three out of four people that
> condition changes itself spontaneously. So if you put
> students into an environment which normalizes homo-
> sexuality, you're going to support the gay identification
> and you will be supporting the wrong thing in three out
> of four instances. That's with no outside intervention,
> just the natural processes of development.[29]

In other words, teenagers pressured by peers, the media, or the schools into declaring their sexuality do so much too soon. Yet many teenagers naturally assume (because of all the messages from the media and our culture) that if they have had one homosexual experience, they must be gay. Statistical surveys such as the one just mentioned demonstrate that the opposite is true. And it is important to remember that many young people's brains don't finish developing until they are about 25 years old.

It is important to point out that in their preteen years, young people often have an emotional attraction to someone of the same sex. This doesn't mean the attraction is sexual in nature, and it doesn't mean that a boy is gay or a girl is lesbian. We usually learn to attach to someone of the same sex before we learn to attach to someone of the opposite sex. This is a normal step in the process of maturation.

However, conflicting messages from the media and society can create confusing feelings within young people about such emotional attraction. Children insecure in their masculinity or femininity may even begin to seek affirmation and affection from someone of the same sex. Sometimes this includes a sexual encounter.

That doesn't mean that these children are homosexual, and it doesn't mean they need to be adopted by the gay groups within the school. Instead, they should be affirmed and encouraged to continue developing their masculinity or femininity in a healthy way.

Because of the rising popularity of various gay groups on campus, many teenagers are prematurely or incorrectly identifying themselves as gay or lesbian. Among some in their peer group, such a declaration is considered cool and radical. And when these teens act on their emotional feelings and experiment with homosexual sex, this "confirms" to them that they have this sexual orientation. A sexual experiment, however, is very different than a sexual orientation. As seen in the aforementioned survey, sexual experiments do not necessarily determine a person's sexual future.

What about the issue of adoption by homosexual parents?

The headlines of the popular press give the impression there is essentially no difference between children who are raised by heterosexual parents and children raised by homosexual parents. And a technical report printed in the journal *Pediatrics* concluded, "A growing body of scientific literature demonstrates that children who grow up with 1 or 2 gay or lesbian parents fare as well in emotional, cognitive, social, and sexual functioning as do children whose parents are heterosexual."[30]

But it turns out the story isn't quite that simple. First, there is abundant evidence to demonstrate that the ideal home in which to raise children includes both a father and a mother. "An extensive body of research tells us that children do best when they grow up with both biological parents," conclude two researchers. They go on to say that "it is not simply the presence of two parents, as some have assumed, but the presence of two biological parents that seems to support child development."[31]

This supports other research in the field. "Most researchers now agree that together these studies support the notion that, on average, children do best when raised by their two married, biological parents."[32]

Second, there are good reasons to question the claim made in the journal *Pediatrics*. This "Technical Report" actually "came from a small eight-member committee within the AAP [American Academy of Pediatrics], and not the larger membership. In fact, this report brought the strongest negative reaction the AAP has ever received from its membership on any issue."[33] In an earlier study, the lead author of the "Technical Report" admitted that research on children raised in homosexual households had limitations, "including small sample size, non-random subject selection, narrow range of socioeconomic and racial background, and lack of long-term longitudinal follow-up."[34]

Other researchers agree. They have found that "studies on same-sex parenting are plagued with persistent limitation[s]." They therefore conclude that "we cannot be confident concerning the generalizability of many of the findings."[35]

At present, it is probably too early to make the confident claims found in the "Technical Report" published in *Pediatrics*. Based on the extensive research that has been done, it is possible to say that children do best when raised in a home with a father and a mother who are the biological parents.

HOMOSEXUALITY
AND THE SCHOOLS

THE PROMOTION OF HOMOSEXUALITY in public schools has become increasingly common. Gay activists and even educators see this as a civil rights issue. Others see it as a safety issue. And these tactics have been successful—who would be against making the public schools a safer environment?

Many of the school and university programs that are used to promote the homosexual agenda spread myths about the homosexual lifestyle. That's why it is important to know the truth about homosexual behavior.

What are some of the myths being spread about homosexuality?

Students hear lots of false information about homosexuality from media and education. Here we will look at four common myths that are often repeated in school programs promoting the gay lifestyle.[1] It is important to know what they are and how to respond to them.

Myth #1: "Homosexuality is normal and healthy."

This is simply not true. Basic biology contradicts this. Males and females were designed to complement each other both physically and psychologically.

Engaging in homosexual behavior is not a healthy activity. Numerous studies show that those students who do engage in homosexual behavior are a much greater risk for sexually transmitted diseases, including AIDS; alcoholism and drug abuse; depression; emotionally exhausting relationships; and a shortened lifespan.[2]

Myth #2: "If you're attracted to someone of the same sex, then that means you're gay or lesbian."

Having feelings toward someone of the opposite sex does not necessarily mean you are homosexual. Rather, it may reveal certain unmet needs for love and attention. These should have been met earlier in life but were not. Having emotional feelings toward other people, of both sexes, is also a normal part of adolescent development, a normal part of transitioning emotionally from childhood to adulthood.

Myth #3: "You were born gay, so you can't change."

As we will see in the next chapter, there is no scientific evidence that anyone is born gay. This claim has been made so often that most people tend to believe it. But the evidence of science contradicts the first assumption. Christian counseling also contradicts this conclusion. Thousands of people who were once gay have experienced real and significant changes in their attractions and behavior.[3] Change in sexual feelings *is* possible.

Myth #4: "Embrace your homosexuality because gay life is cool."

For many homosexuals, the gay lifestyle is not gay (fun). Those in ministry to homosexuals have heard many heartbreaking stories about the dark side of intense and difficult relationships, relational patterns of disillusionment and breakups, and physical and emotional unhealthiness. Countless people say they wish they had never entered the gay community in the first place, but they often find it hard to leave.

How is the gay agenda advanced in public schools?

Since the early 1990s gay activists and various homosexual groups have worked hard to gain greater access to public schools. Usually the focus of their efforts is upon making schools a safer place for gay, lesbian, bisexual, transgender, and transsexual students—thereby justifying the introduction of materials and speakers on the subject of homosexuality. And the establishment of homosexual clubs on campuses provides a platform for introducing and promoting homosexuality to students.

Two key organizations active in this regard are the Gay, Lesbian and Straight Education Network (GLSEN) and Parents, Families and Friends of Lesbians and Gays (PFLAG). Both have helped prohomosexual speakers, programs, and curricula gain a foothold in schools.

Perhaps the most effective wedge used by gay activists to open the door to the public schools has been concern over student safety. Kevin Jennings, the executive director for GLSEN, explained in a speech how the "safety" issue was a most effective strategy:

> In Massachusetts, the effective reframing of this issue was the key to the success of the Governor's Commission on Gay and Lesbian Youth. We immediately seized upon the opponent's calling card—safety—and explained how homophobia represents a threat to students' safety by creating a climate where violence, name-calling, health problems, and suicide are common. Titling our report "Making Schools Safe for Gay and Lesbian Youth," we automatically threw our opponents onto the defensive and stole their best line of attack.

This framing short-circuited their arguments and left them back-pedaling from day one.[4]

The strategy has obviously been successful because no one would want to be against creating a safer environment in public schools. It almost doesn't matter whether the allegations are true. Once you raise the concern of safety, most administrators, teachers, and parents quickly fall in line and cooperate with gay activists.

There is an irony in all of this. Many of the behaviors that are taught and affirmed in these school programs and clubs are unsafe in terms of public health. For example, *Pediatrics* (journal of the American Academy of Pediatrics) reported on a Harvard study that found more than 30 risks positively associated with self-reported gay-lesbian-bisexual (GLB) orientation.[5] So it is indeed ironic that the idea of "safety" is often used as a means to introduce the teaching and discussion of behaviors that have been proven to be quite unsafe.

A lesson plan in the San Francisco Unified School District for kindergarteners and first graders redefines families in an effort to promote homosexuality. It is called "My Family" and is distributed through the district's Support Services for Gay, Lesbian, and Bisexual Youth Department. It defines a family as a "unit of two or more persons, related either by birth or by choice, who may or may not live together, who try to meet each other's needs and share common goals and interests."[6]

Another effective strategy has been the formation of gay clubs on campuses. More than 3000 such clubs have been formed in high schools (and some middle schools) around the nation. They provide a platform for information distribution and even recruitment on public school campuses.

What are the goals of GLSEN?

The mission statement of GLSEN is straightforward: "The Gay, Lesbian & Straight Education Network strives to assure that each member of every school community is valued and respected regardless of sexual orientation or gender identity/expression."[7] It is a growing, well-funded homosexual organization that promotes homosexual identity and behavior on campus. It has been very successful in gaining access on campuses by working with such influential groups as the National Education Association.

Anyone who takes the time to read some of the materials recommended by GLSEN will quickly find that it condones sexual themes and information that would be disturbing to most parents. One researcher who has taken the time to review these materials and investigate various school programs came to the following seven conclusions:[8]

1. GLSEN believes the early sexualization of children can be beneficial. This means that virtually any sexual activity—as well as exposure to graphic sexual images and material—is not just permissible but good for children as part of the process of discovering their sexuality.

2. "Coming out" (calling oneself or believing oneself to be homosexual) and even beginning homosexual sex practices at a young age is a normal and positive experience for youth that should be encouraged by teachers and parents, according to GLSEN.

3. Bisexuality, "fluid" sexuality, and sexual experimentation is encouraged by GLSEN as a right for all students.

4. Meeting other "gay" and "questioning" youth, sometimes without parental knowledge, is a frequent theme

in GLSEN materials. At these meetings, minors will come into contact with college-age people and adults who practice homosexuality.

5. In GLSEN material, the "cool" adults, parents, teachers, and counselors are those who encourage students to embrace homosexuality and cross-dress. They also allow adult-level freedoms and let children associate with questionable teens or adults.

6. GLSEN resources contain many hostile, one-sided, anti-Christian vignettes and opinions as well as false information about Christianity and the Bible's position on homosexuality. This encourages antagonism against biblical morality and increases the risk that youth will experiment with high-risk behavior. It also increases prejudice against Christians and Jews.

7. The spirituality presented positively in GLSEN resources is heavily laced with occult themes and nightmarish images.

Each of these seven conclusions was documented by the researcher with paragraphs and footnotes of examples.

What are the goals of PFLAG?

PFLAG is a national organization of parents, families, and friends that "promotes the health and well-being of gay, lesbian, bisexual and transgender persons."[9] This organization actively promotes, at the local level, its views of human sexuality in schools, churches, and various youth organizations. Although there is a strong emphasis on rights and tolerance, PFLAG's message about sexuality would disturb most parents. A researcher who has taken the time to review their brochures and other materials came to the following five conclusions:[10]

1. PFLAG believes in total sexual license for people of all ages. This means that virtually any sexual activity as well as exposure to graphic sexual images and material is not just permissible but *good for children* as part of the process of discovering their sexuality.

2. "Coming out" (calling oneself homosexual or cross-dressing) at a very young age, and even beginning homosexual sex practices at an early age, is a desirable goal in the world, according to PFLAG.

3. Bisexuality, fluid sexuality, and sexual experimentation is encouraged by PFLAG. The group believes it's important for *all* students to learn about these options.

4. Meeting with other "gay" and "questioning" youth, usually without parental knowledge, is a frequent theme in PFLAG materials. At these community meetings, 13-year-olds come into contact with college-age youth and adults who practice homosexuality.

5. PFLAG spreads false information about the Bible, religious faith, and the restoration of heterosexuality through faith. This misinformation closes the door of change for many young people and stirs up anti-Christian and anti-Jewish bias and hostility.

What are the goals of gay clubs?

In the mid-1990s, there were a few dozen Gay-Straight Alliance (GSA) clubs in U.S. high schools. Today there are 3200 registered clubs.[11]

A Gay-Straight Alliance (GSA) is a student-run club that provides a meeting place for student talk about homosexuality and homosexual behaviors. It is also provides a platform for outside speakers to address various topics and for students to organize a "Pride Week" on campus.

Some GSA clubs might organize a "Teach the Teacher" day, during which faculty are told how they can be more understanding of gay, lesbian, bisexual, transgender, or transsexual students. Once a year, many of the students in these clubs also participate in "The Day of Silence." On this day, the students stay silent as a way of acknowledging the silence induced by those who oppose homosexuality.

Administrators and teachers who are approached by students who want to form a gay club should know about what may take place in that club based upon the past behavior of other such clubs. One researcher uncovered the following seven common trends among these gay clubs: [12]

1. Misinformation favorable to homosexuality is disseminated

2. The students' "rights" to "be who they are"—i.e., to participate in homosexual behavior—is constantly reinforced

3. Constant emphasis on what the group believes constitutes harassment or discrimination by other students or teachers

4. Encouragement toward activism and activist training

5. Traditional religions that disapprove of homosexuality are regularly trashed

6. Cross-dressing and even sex-change surgery are said to be defensible activities for teens

7. Social activities are planned for homosexual teens— and their adult advisors

What is the potential legal liability of homosexual education?

Is there any legal liability when schools permit and even promote homosexual education on a campus? One group (Citizens for Community Values) believes there is a potential liability. This group has published a manual documenting the potential liability that schools, administrators, and teachers might face. They argue that the "safe school" message of many of these homosexual groups "is nothing more than a deceptive ploy designed to preach safety while actually encouraging sexual behaviors that are quite unsafe."[13]

Their argument rests on the following assumption: A legal liability (a tort of negligence) exists when school officials grant gay activist groups access to students and those same students subsequently suffer physical or mental harm. A tort of negligence exists when: (1) there is a duty or obligation to protect another from unreasonable risk, (2) there is a failure to observe that duty, (3) there is a causal connection between the failure and the alleged injury, and (4) actual loss or damage has taken place.

Is there potential for physical and mental health risks when homosexual education is promoted within the schools? As we have already noted in the previous chapter, there are studies that indicate that certain risks can and do occur when an individual engages in homosexual behavior. The following is a brief summary of much more information that can be found in the document "The Legal Liability Associated with Homosexual Education in Public Schools."[14]

Life expectancy—The *International Journal of Epidemiology* found that gay and bisexual men involved in homosexual behavior cut off years from their lives. One study showed:

> In a major Canadian centre, life expectancy at age 20 years for gay and bisexual men is 8 to 20 years less than

for all men. If the same pattern of mortality were to continue, we estimate that nearly half of gay and bisexual men currently aged 20 years will not reach their 65th birthday. Under even the most liberal assumptions, gay and bisexual men in this urban centre are now experiencing a life expectancy similar to that experienced by all men in Canada in the year 1871.[15]

Sexually transmitted diseases—The danger of various STDs, including HIV infection, has been well documented through many studies. This statement by the Medical Institute for Sexual Health provides a good summary of the various STD risks in homosexual relationships:

Homosexual men are at significantly increased risk of HIV/AIDS, hepatitis, anal cancer, gonorrhea and gastrointestinal infections as a result of their sexual practices. Women who have sex with women are at significantly increased risk of bacterial vaginosis, breast cancer and ovarian cancer than are heterosexual women.[16]

Other health risk behaviors—A study by Harvard University of over 4000 ninth- to twelfth-grade students found that gay-lesbian-bisexual "youth report disproportionate risk for a variety of health risk and problem behaviors." The study found that such youth "engage in twice the mean number of risk behaviors as did the overall population."[17]

Mental health—A study published in the *Archives of General Psychiatry* found that those who engage in homosexual behavior have a much higher incidence of mental health problems. "The findings support the assumption that people with same-sex sexual behavior are at greater risk for psychiatric disorders."[18]

Permitting and promoting homosexual activity through on-campus programs and clubs will certainly increase homosexual behavior among students. Administrators, teachers, and parents should reconsider the impact these programs, and the subsequent behavior, will have on the student body.

How is the gay agenda promoted at universities?

At a time when college costs have gone through the roof, many wonder if students and their parents are getting their money's worth with some of the rather unusual courses being taught.[19] Some of these courses lend themselves to the promotion of the gay agenda.

For example, an Occidental College course called The Phallus covers a broad study on the relation "between the phallus and the penis, the meaning of the phallus, phallologocentrism, the lesbian phallus, the Jewish phallus, the Latino phallus, and the relation of the phallus and fetishism." Students at the University of Pennsylvania can take a course on adultery novels and read a series of nineteenth- and twentieth-century works about adultery and watch "several adultery films." And students at University of Michigan can study the development of "Native feminist thought" and its "relationship both to Native land-based struggles and non-Native feminist movements."

There are also classes that specifically focus on homosexuality and gay studies. UCLA offers a course called Queer Musicology, which explores how "sexual difference and complex gender identities in music and among musicians have incited productive consternation" during the 1990s. Music under consideration includes works by Schubert and Holly Near, Britten and Cole Porter, and Pussy Tourette.

University of California at Berkeley has a class called Sex Change City: Theorizing History in Genderqueer San Francisco, which explores "implications of U.S. imperialism and colonization for the construction of gender in 19th-century San Francisco's multicultural, multiracial, and multiethnic" community. The course also covers "contemporary transgender, queer, genderqueer, and post-queer cultural production and politics" and "the regulation of gender-variant practices in public space by San Francisco's Anglo-European elites."

University of Colorado-Boulder students can take the course Introduction to Lesbian, Bisexual, and Gay Literature. It introduces some of the forms, concerns, and genres of contemporary lesbian, bisexual, and gay writing in English. Hollins University's course Lesbian Pulp Fiction examines "a literary genre that critics once deemed 'trash' and moralists commonly found 'scandalous,' but that formed a crucial part in the burgeoning canon of queer literature."

Courses and professors promoting homosexuality and the gay lifestyle can be found on nearly every college campus. What is unfortunate is that these courses displace valuable course material that used to be part of a university education. All of this is taking place at a time when only one in four Americans can name more than one of the five freedoms protected by the First Amendment.[20] By contrast, more than half can name at least two family members on *The Simpsons*.

Even more astounding is the report in *The Washington Post* that only 31 percent of college grads could read and comprehend complex books.[21] It doesn't appear that the classes on lesbian, bisexual, and gay literature are helping university students become more proficient in reading and comprehension.

THE CAUSES OF HOMOSEXUALITY

Open a newspaper or turn on a television program, and you are likely to read or hear someone say that homosexuals are born with that sexual orientation. An expert might cite studies done on the brains of cadavers or with gay twins. Another expert might talk about a "gay gene." So is there a biological cause for homosexuality?

Another important question is whether there are psychological causes of homosexuality. Are there certain family and social conditions that influence sexual orientation and shape homosexual desire? These are difficult questions that elicit all different kinds of responses from people. What do we really know for sure?

Is there a biological cause for homosexuality?

The answer is not as simple as homosexual activists and the popular press would have us believe. Many factors influence human sexuality. Providing a single cause for homosexuality is impossible. No "typical homosexual" exists, and it is doubtful that we will ever find a single causal factor for homosexuality. Physiological, psychological, and spiritual factors all play a part.

For years scientists have been looking for biological causes for homosexuality. Finding such a factor (hormones or a gay gene) would give support to the frequently heard homosexual cliché that "I was born this way." It would give credence to the concept that homosexuality is not a sin but a biological condition entitled to legal and social recognition.[1]

There are researchers who have published a variety of studies to show a correlation between sexual orientation and brain structure, genetic structure, finger length, eye blinking, hormonal differentiation, etc. The three most prominent studies in this regard have been a brain study by Simon LeVay, a twins study by Michael Bailey and Richard Pillard, and a genetic study by Dean Hamer.

Simon LeVay, a neuroscientist at the Salk Institute, argued that homosexuals and heterosexuals have notable differences in the structure of their brains. In 1991 he studied 41 cadavers (19 homosexual men, 16 heterosexual men, and 6 heterosexual women). He found that a specific portion of the hypothalamus, the area of the brain that, among other things, governs sexual activity, was consistently smaller in homosexuals than in heterosexuals.[2] This led him to argue that there is a distinct physiological component to sexual orientation. In other words, "biology is destiny."

Numerous problems exist with this study, however. First, there was considerable range in the sizes of the hypothalamic region in the subjects. In a few homosexual men this region was the same size as that of the heterosexuals, and in a few heterosexuals this region was as small as that of the homosexuals. So the statistical correlation is not as strong as news reports of the initial study might lead one to believe.

Second is the chicken-and-egg problem. When there is a difference in brain structure, is the difference the *cause* of one's sexual orientation, or is it the *result* of one's sexual behavior? Researchers, for example, have found that when people who become blind begin to learn Braille, the area of the brain that controls the reading finger grows larger. Could there be a similar explanation for the size difference between the hypothalami of homosexuals and heterosexuals?

Third, LeVay later admitted that he did not know the sexual orientation of some of the cadavers in the study. He acknowledged that he was not sure if the heterosexual males in the study were actually heterosexual. Since some of those he identified as heterosexual died of AIDS, critics have raised doubts about the accuracy of his study.

Fourth, there was the potential for bias in the study. LeVay has said he was driven to study the potential physiological roots of homosexuality after his homosexual lover died of AIDS. He even admitted that if he failed to find a genetic cause for homosexuality that he might walk away from science altogether.[3] Later he did just that by moving to West Hollywood to open up a small, unaccredited "study center" focusing on homosexuality.

In December 1991, Michael Bailey of Northwestern University joined Richard Pillard of the Boston University School of Medicine in publishing a study about homosexuality in twins.[4] They surveyed homosexual men about their brothers and discovered what they believe proved that sexual orientation is biological. Of the homosexuals who had identical twin brothers, 52 percent of those twins were also homosexual. Of those who had fraternal twins, 22 percent said that their twin was gay, and only 11 percent of those who had adopted siblings said that their adopted brothers were also homosexual. Bailey and Pillard attributed the differences in those percentages to the differences in genetic material shared.

Though this study has been touted as proving a genetic basis to homosexuality, it contained significant flaws. First, Bailey and Pillard's theory is not new. It was first proposed in 1952. Since that time three other separate studies have come to different conclusions.[5] Therefore, the conclusions of the Bailey–Pillard study should be considered in the light of other contradictory studies.

Second, most published reports did not mention that only 9 percent of the nontwin brothers of homosexuals were homosexuals. Fraternal twins share no more genetic material than nontwin brothers, yet homosexuals are more than twice as likely to share their sexual orientation with a fraternal twin than with a nontwin brother. Whatever the reason, the answer cannot be genetic.

Third, why are not nearly all identical twin brothers of homosexuals also homosexual? In other words, if biology is determinative, why are nearly half the identical twins not homosexual? Bailey admitted that "there must be something in the environment to yield the discordant twins."[6] And that is precisely the point; there is something (perhaps everything) in the environment to explain sexual orientation.

Could the social and emotional closeness of twins explain similar sexual orientation? An identical twin of a homosexual who sleeps in the same bed or bedroom is more apt to be physically closer to his twin. As one biologist put it, "In order for such a study to be at all meaningful, you'd have to look at twins raised apart. It's such badly interpreted genetics."[7]

Fourth, there was potential for bias in the twins study. Bailey is a homosexual and has been an outspoken proponent of a progay agenda in science. While the study should be evaluated on its merits, it is important to be aware of potential bias in any scientific study.

What about the news about the discovery of a gay gene?

In the early 1990s, the media promoted the idea that there was a gay gene that determined whether a person would be homosexual. A team of researchers led by Dean Hamer of the National Cancer Institute announced "preliminary" findings from research into the connection between homosexuality and genetic inheritance.[8] In a sample of 76 homosexual males, the researchers found a statistically higher incidence of homosexuality in their male relatives (brothers, uncles) on their mother's side of the family, which suggested a possible inherited link through the X chromosome. A follow-up study of 40 pairs of homosexual brothers found that 33 of the pairs shared a variation in a small section of the chromosome region known as Xq28.

Although the press promoted this study as evidence of a gay gene, some of the same concerns raised with the previous two studies apply here. First, the findings involve a limited sample size and are therefore sketchy. Even the researchers acknowledged that these were "preliminary" findings. In addition to the sample size being small, the researchers did no control testing for heterosexual brothers. Critics also raised questions about the insufficient research done on the social histories of the homosexuals' families.

Second, similarity does not prove cause. Just because 33 pairs of homosexual brothers share a genetic variation does not mean that variation causes homosexuality. And what about the other seven pairs that did not show the variation but were homosexuals? Some of the same concerns raised about the Bailey–Pillard study are relevant here.

Third, research bias may again be an issue. Hamer and at least one of his other research team members are homosexual, a fact which apparently was deliberately kept from the press and was not revealed until later. Hamer, it turns out, is not merely an objective observer. He has presented himself as an expert witness on homosexuality and has stated that he hopes that his research would give comfort to men feeling guilty about their homosexuality.[9]

Each of these three studies looking for a biological cause for homosexuality has its flaws. Does that mean there is no physiological component to homosexuality? Not at all. Actually, it is probably too early to say conclusively. Scientists may indeed discover a clear biological predisposition to sexual orientation. But a predisposition is not the same thing as a determination. Maintaining this difference leads to some key distinctions, according to Sherwood Cole:

> Assuming that biological influences on homosexuality are "predisposing" rather than "determining" also allows one to make some additional important distinctions. For example, "predisposing" influences are much more likely to influence one's orientation (desires, attitudes, preferences, attractions, and fantasies) than one's behavior. While these influences are not to be treated lightly, it may or may not result in the overt expression of homosexual behavior. Since the Bible's condemnation and prohibition of homosexuality (Lev. 18:22; 20:13; Rom. 1:26-27; 1 Cor. 6:9; 1 Tim. 1:10) address behavioral practices, not orientation, this distinction is important to the debate. The individual who, in spite of a homosexual orientation, refrains from the practice of this lifestyle is to be commended, not condemned.[10]

The social and moral implications of this distinction are also relevant. Some people may inherit a predisposition for anger, depression, or alcoholism, yet society does not condone these behaviors. And even if violence, depression, or alcoholism were proven to be inborn (determined by genetic material), would we accept them as normal and refuse to treat them? Of course not. The Bible has clear statements about how we should view such things as anger and alcoholism. Likewise, the Bible has clear statements about how we should view homosexuality.

Is homosexuality just about sex?

Obviously homosexuality involves sex. But sex is really only a small part of homosexuality. Certainly there is sexual attraction and there is a degree of sexual intimacy, but the larger issue is the emotional need of the person seeking a sexual experience from someone of the same gender.

People seeking a homosexual experience are often looking for love, affirmation, and acceptance. These are legitimate desires that a gay or lesbian is attempting to fulfill in an illegitimate way. The sexual encounter is a by-product.

This is especially true for those who get involved in a sexual encounter before puberty. They aren't looking for sex. They may be experimenting. They may be looking for intimacy. But they aren't looking for sex at a prepubescent age.

What are the psychological causes of homosexuality?

Because human sexuality is so complex, the possibility of finding a single cause for homosexuality is unlikely. There is, however, growing evidence that a number of environmental factors in a family or an individual's experience seems to influence one's sexual orientation.

Since the time of Sigmund Freud, counselors have noticed a pattern of family relationships that frequently appears in a homosexual's family of origin: a domineering mother and a passive or absent father. Though this is a stereotype with obvious exceptions, the pattern still manifests itself in the lives of many homosexual men. One counselor summarized the various research findings in this way:

> In his book *Male Homosexuality*...Dr. Richard Friedman cites 13 independent studies from 1959 to 1981 on the early family lives of homosexuals. Out of these 13, all

but one concluded that, in the parent-child interactions of adult homosexuals, the subject's relationship with the parent of the same sex was unsatisfactory, ranging from a distant, nonintimate relationship to an outright hostile one.[11]

Another psychological factor is early sexual experience. Many homosexuals cite backgrounds of being sexually molested or having had sexual experiences early in their childhood. These experiences may range from sexual abuse (from another homosexual

---

Point of View: Are there any common factors associated with homosexuality?

Dr. Nicolosi: I do this work almost exclusively. We have 135 cases a week and have treated over a thousand men. I can tell you that we find the "classic triadic relationship." It's like a triangle. In one corner, you have the overinvolved, intrusive, domineering mother. In the other corner you have the passive, avoidant, hostile father. And in the other corner you have the temperamentally introverted, sensitive, artistic, timid boy.

That's the classic triadic relationship. Mother and father did not get along, did not have good communication. This occurs when the boy goes through the gender identity phase [around 1½ to 3 years old]. The mother and son have a particularly close relationship. The father and son have a particularly alienated or detached relationship.

That pattern we see over and over again almost without exception. To add to that, if there is an older brother, there is usually a feared, hostile relationship.

—Interview with **Dr. Joseph Nicolosi**
on *Point of View* radio talk show[12]

---

or a family member) to an early childhood sexual experience that could be described as pleasurable. In an attempt to rationalize the feelings that surface from this experience, the child often begins to act on those feelings and pursue similar sexual experimentation.

Much less research has been done on lesbians, but sexual abuse does seem to be a frequent pattern in the history of women with homosexual tendencies. This abuse may be physical, sexual, or emotional. When the abuse comes from a man, the woman may view men as tyrants and avoid them. When the abuse comes from a woman, she may grow up longing for womanly love and protection she did not receive in her younger years.

Psychologists have identified certain emotional needs that all people share in common, and homosexuals report that for them, one or more of these emotional needs have gone unmet.[13] Is it possible that homosexuals attempt to meet these legitimate needs in biblically illegitimate ways that manifest themselves in their sexual patterns? Three emotional needs are relevant to this discussion.

The first emotional need every person has is the need for gender identity. In other words, what does it mean to be male or female? Boys with gender identity problems do not feel masculine. For a boy to show effeminate behavior is not femininity; it is a lack of confidence in his ability to be masculine. Often this behavior derives from a lack of bonding with the same-sex parent ("I'm unacceptable to my father, so I must be unacceptable to other males"). For lesbians, the trigger will be the opposite. Whereas the trigger for the male can be a weak father, the trigger for a female may be a distant mother.

The second emotional need is for a healthy role model. How does an emotionally healthy man or woman act? Children learn what masculinity and femininity are by watching how proper sexuality is modeled in the lives of those close to them. When the role models are missing, the cues and influences may be missing or mixed, thereby leading to a different sense of identity and sexual orientation.

The third emotional need is for same-sex bonding. Bonding with members of one's own sex is a basic psychological need that would include bonding with a nurturer (usually a parent), a mentor (a coach, a teacher, a discipler), and comrades (peers and friends of the same sex). Research shows that only after bonding with the same sex has been fulfilled can relationships move on to the opposite sex. For some, however, bonding with others of the same sex does not happen. A boy, for example, may bond with the women in his life, or with no one at all. Some counselors suggest that people struggling with homosexual feelings are not so much having a sexual problem as much as they are having a relational problem. This same-sex "deficit" may be an explanation for homosexual behavior.

What are the spiritual causes of homosexuality?

Ultimately homosexuality is a manifestation of the sin nature that strikes us all (Romans 3:23). Because of mankind's fall into sin (Genesis 3), God's creation was spoiled and human behavior has fallen into degrading passions (Romans 1:24). Sin has spoiled every aspect of our being (spiritual, intellectual, emotional, physical, sexual). Therefore, we should not be surprised that anyone could have sexual desires that are wrong. Those who choose to act on those feelings and temptations are acting outside God's plan for human sexuality.

A society that turns from God's plan accelerates sexual irresponsibility. Homosexuals are told they "were born that way" and should celebrate their sexuality. Heterosexuals are encouraged to experiment and expand their sexual choices. People with guilt feelings over their sexual experiences and temptations are encouraged to accept their feelings with the cliché "Once gay, always gay." The ultimate problem is not physiological or even psychological, but an unwillingness to deal with the spiritual problem of sin. Psychological and spiritual counsel, therefore, is the answer to homosexuality.

Is it possible for homosexuals to change their orientation?

One of the most frequent clichés heard in homosexual circles is "Once gay, always gay." In a sense it is a corollary cliché to the slogan "You are born gay." Secular counselors routinely tell patients struggling with homosexual feelings that they were born that way, that they cannot change, and that they should simply learn to affirm their feelings.

Despite such clichés and counseling there is hope for the person struggling with homosexual feelings. Groups such as Exodus International provide a network of 90 organizations that specialize in helping homosexuals leave their lifestyle and change their sexual orientation. Consider this sampling of quotations from experts in the sexual counseling field:

- "Some people do change their sexual orientation."[14]

- "Despite the rhetoric of homosexual activists, all studies which have attempted conversion from homosexuality to heterosexuality have had significant success."[15]

- "I have recently had occasion to review the result of psychotherapy with homosexuals and have been surprised by the findings—a considerable percentage of overt homosexuals became heterosexual."[16]

The National Institute of Mental Health states that over 50 percent of homosexually oriented individuals who present themselves for treatment can be helped to become heterosexual.[17] According to Dr. Charles Socarides, formerly a professor at Albert Einstein College of Medicine, "There is at present sufficient evident that in a majority of cases homosexuality can be successfully treated in psychoanalysis."[18]

Perhaps one of the most definitive statements on the matter of change has come from an unlikely source. In 1973, Robert Switzer, professor of psychiatry at Columbia University, was instrumental in removing homosexuality from the American Psychiatric Association's list of mental disorders. He wrote a study published in the October 2003 *Archives of Sexual Behavior* contending that people can change their "sexual orientation" from homosexual to heterosexual.[19]

Recent press reports, as well as academic studies, suggest that sexual preference among young teen women is very fluid and influenced by choice and cultural circumstances. According to Laura Sessions Stepp, "Recent studies among women suggest that female homosexuality may be grounded more in social interaction, may present itself as an emotional attraction in addition to or in place of a physical one, and may change over time."[20]

Lisa Diamond of the University of Utah conducted a longitudinal study of women (ages 16 to 23) who were attracted to other women. She found that nearly two-thirds changed their sexual labels during the period the study took place.[21]

The success rate for homosexuals who receive counseling for changing their sexual orientation varies, given the different approaches and circumstances. William Masters and Virginia Johnson reported successful results in 71.6 percent of all cases after a six-year follow-up period.[22] Others have also reported success rates in that range.

Ultimately it is Christ's loving act of redemption that can free someone bound by the ropes of sexual addiction (heterosexual or homosexual). Some people experience no further homosexual temptations, but most struggle with their sexual temptations in the process of sanctification (spiritual growth). Individual Christians and churches must find creative ways to reach out to those caught in the bondage of homosexuality by learning to love the sinner while hating the sin.

If people believe that you are born gay, does that affect their perception about homosexuality?

What difference does it make if you believe that homosexuality is genetic? There appears to be a big difference in perception and subsequent attitudes. A 2006 poll done by the Pew Research Center demonstrated that 55 percent of Americans oppose same-sex marriage, while 33 percent support it.[23]

The poll also found a very strong correlation between the view that homosexuality is innate and support for gay marriage. For example, 58 percent of the respondents who believed that a person is born homosexual also supported a redefinition of marriage to include same-sex couples. By contrast, of those who believed that homosexuality is acquired, over 70 percent opposed a redefinition of marriage.

The conclusions are understandable. If you believe that people are born homosexual, then it is likely that you will classify sexual orientation in the same way that you classify race or gender or other innate characteristics. Thus, you would be more likely to argue for a redefinition of marriage to include same-sex couples.

This conclusion, however, does not necessarily follow. As we have already shown, there are some questions about whether the origins of homosexuality are genetic. But, for the sake of argument, let's assume some studies are able to show there is a genetic component to homosexuality. These studies would tell us something about the *origin* of homosexuality, but they would not tell us anything about the *morality* of homosexuality. We are all born with a sin nature (Romans 3:23), but that does not mean that we should condone all sinful behavior. The origin of a behavior and the morality of a behavior are two different issues.

Consider the following: Some people believe there is a genetic component to alcoholism. Would that mean we should encourage people to drink alcohol and become drunk? That is not what the apostle Paul says in Ephesians 5:18: "Do not get drunk with wine, for that is dissipation, but be filled with the Spirit."

Some people believe there may be a genetic component to anger. But that doesn't mean we should affirm the behaviors of being easily angered and lashing out at others. Paul wrote in Ephesians 4:26, "Be angry, and yet do not sin; do not let the sun go down on your anger."

It is understandable that people might change their minds about homosexuality if they believe that it is innate. One conservative editor admitted that he used to hold to a certain view about gays and lesbians based upon his religious convictions. But he changed those views when he became convinced that homosexuality was genetic.[24]

But, as explained above, there are likely genetic components to other actions and behaviors that are unbiblical. That does not mean we should encourage people to act on such feelings and temptations.

HOMOSEXUALITY AND THE BIBLE

OVER THE LAST FEW DECADES, many churches and denominations have attempted to reinterpret the biblical passages that deal with homosexuality. In the past, liberal theologians merely stated that the Bible was written by authors who were intent on promoting their ethical and religious bias. Therefore, whatever the Bible had to say about homosexuality was irrelevant.

Now there are churches and theologians who claim they believe in the authority of the Bible but argue that the biblical passages concerning homosexuality have been misinterpreted. Whole books and theological articles have been written on this, so we cannot begin to cover all the arguments. But here are a few key arguments we can examine and respond to.

What does the Old Testament say about homosexuality?

The first mention of homosexuality in the Bible is in Genesis 19. Lot entertained two angels who came to the city of Sodom to investigate its sins. In the evening all the men from every part of the city surrounded Lot's house and ordered him to bring out the visitors so that "we may know them" (19:5 NKJV). The

Hebrew word for "know" (*yadah*) means that the men of the city wanted to have sex with the visitors, which is why many modern translations render the phrase "so that they may have relations with them" or "so that we can have sex with them."

Proponents of homosexuality argue that biblical commentators misunderstand the story of Sodom.[1] They argue that the men of the city merely wanted to meet these visitors. They wanted to extend Middle Eastern hospitality to those who were in Lot's house. They say the sin of Sodom was inhospitality, not homosexuality.

Prohomosexuality commentators point out that the Hebrew word *yadah* can mean "to get acquainted with" as well as "to have intercourse with." In fact, the word appears over 900 times in the Old Testament, and only 12 times does it mean "to have sex with" someone. So they conclude that the sin of Sodom had nothing to do with homosexuality.

The problem with this argument is the context of the Scripture passage. Statistics should not be given more weight than exegesis. Word count alone is not the sole criterion for determining the meaning of words. And even if a statistical count should be used, the argument backfires. Of the 12 times the phrase "to know" is used in the book of Genesis, it does mean "to have intercourse with" in 10 of the 12 occurrences.

The context of the passage does not warrant the interpretation that the men of Sodom only wanted to get acquainted with the strangers. This is borne out by Lot's reply in Genesis 19:6-8:

> Lot went out to them at the doorway, and shut the door behind him, and said, "Please, my brothers, do not act wickedly. Now behold, I have two daughters who have not had relations with man; please let me bring them out to you, and do to them whatever you like; only do nothing to these men, inasmuch as they have come under the shelter of my roof."

One can sense Lot's panic as he foolishly offered his virgin daughters to the crowd instead of the foreign men. This is not the action of a man responding to a crowd's request to merely become acquainted with others.

Lot described his daughters as women who have not had relations with a man. Clearly this statement implies sexual intercourse and does not mean "to be acquainted with." It is unlikely that the first use *yadah* (verse 5) differs from the second use (verse 8). In both instances, *yadah* means "to have intercourse with" or "to have sex with." This is the only consistent translation for the passage.

In the New Testament, in Jude 7, we find a a fitting commentary on Genesis 19. This passage clearly states that the sin of Sodom involved "sexual immorality and perversion" (NIV). The word "perversion" could imply homosexuality or even bestiality, and provides further evidence that the sin of Sodom was homosexuality, not inhospitality.

If the Mosaic law has been abolished, doesn't this invalidate these verses?

Homosexual practices are also condemned in the Mosaic law. Two passages in Leviticus call homosexuality detestable or an abomination: "You shall not lie with a male as one lies with a female; it is an abomination" (18:22), and "If there is a man who lies with a male as those who lie with a woman, both of them have committed a detestable act" (20:13).

Prohomosexual commentators argue that these prohibitions were merely for the Old Testament theocracy in the nation of Israel and are not relevant today. They suggest that if Christians wanted to be consistent with the Old Testament law code in Leviticus, they should avoid eating rare steak, wearing mixed fabrics, and having marital intercourse during a wife's menstrual period.[2]

The logical extension of the argument that the Old Testament admonition against homosexuality is irrelevant today would be that adultery (see Leviticus 18:20) and bestiality (see Leviticus 18:23) and incest (see Leviticus 18:17) are also morally acceptable, since the prohibitions against these sins surround the prohibition against homosexuality.

Even though we no longer observe the ceremonial law, the moral law is still in force. The New Testament speaks of the "law of the Spirit" (Romans 8:2) and the "law of Christ" (Galatians 6:2). We are no longer under the Mosaic law (Galatians 3:17-25) but that does not mean that sin is no longer sin. One cannot say that something that was sin under the law is not sin under grace.

Ceremonial laws concerning diet or wearing mixed fabrics no longer apply today, but moral laws (especially those rooted in God's creation order for human sexuality) most definitely are still relevant. This is especially evident in the fact that prohibitions against homosexuality can also be found in the New Testament.

It's also important to point out that even though the moral law continues to this day, the punishments prescribed in the Old Testament theocracy do not. Homosexuality is still a sin, but the civil punishment for a such sin applies only to the theocratic government in the Old Testament.

What does the New Testament say about homosexuality?

Three key New Testament passages concerning homosexuality are Romans 1:24-27; 1 Corinthians 6:9-11; and 1 Timothy 1:8-10. Of the three, the most significant is Romans 1:24-27 because it deals with homosexuality within the larger cultural context of the Hellenistic world:

> God gave them over in the lusts of their hearts to impurity, so that their bodies would be dishonored among

them. For they exchanged the truth of God for a lie, and worshiped and served the creature rather than the Creator, who is blessed forever. Amen. For this reason God gave them over to degrading passions; for their women exchanged the natural function for that which is unnatural, and in the same way also the men abandoned the natural function of the woman and burned in their desire toward one another, men with men committing indecent acts and receiving in their own persons the due penalty of their error.

Here, Paul talks about people who have turned away from the true worship of God. The result is that "God gave them over to degrading passions." Rather than follow God's instructions for their lives, they "suppress the truth in unrighteousness" (Romans 1:18).

One theologian points out that this passage in Romans is the central biblical text for the topic of homosexual conduct:

This is true for several reasons. It is the most substantial and explicit discussion of the issue in the Bible. It is located in the New Testament. It makes an explicit statement not only about same-sex intercourse among men but also about lesbianism. And it occurs within a substantial corpus of material from a single writer, which allows the interpreter to properly contextualize the writer's stance on homosexuality.[3]

Another New Testament passage dealing with homosexuality is 1 Corinthians 6:9–11. This passage can be a help to those struggling with homosexual temptation to see that change is possible:

Do you not know that the unrighteous will not inherit the kingdom of God? Do not be deceived; neither fornicators, nor idolaters, nor adulterers, nor effeminate,

> nor homosexuals, nor thieves, nor the covetous, nor drunkards, nor revilers, nor swindlers, will inherit the kingdom of God. Such were some of you; but you were washed, but you were sanctified, but you were justified in the name of the Lord Jesus Christ and in the Spirit of our God.

This passage is helpful because it shows that homosexuality is certainly not the greatest sin or an unforgivable sin. Homosexuality is listed with other sins that can keep us from experiencing God's best for our lives. Change is possible ("such were some of you") through salvation and repentance ("but you were sanctified, but you were justified").

Prohomosexual commentators attempt to argue that in this passage, Paul was not addressing homosexuality in general. They say that he was only singling out "homosexual offenders" (since this is how some Bible translations render this passage). In other words, they argue that Paul was condemning homosexual abuse rather than responsible homosexual behavior.

In essence, these commentators suggest that Paul was calling for temperance rather than abstinence. But this approach could not be applied to the other sins listed in 1 Corinthians 6. Was Paul calling for responsible adultery or responsible prostitution? Is there such a thing as moral theft or swindling? Obviously the argument breaks down. Scripture never condones sex outside of heterosexual marriage, and this includes premarital sex, extramarital sex, and homosexual sex.

The third major New Testament passage that addresses homosexuality is 1 Timothy 1:8-10:

> But we know that the Law is good, if one uses it lawfully, realizing the fact that law is not made for a righteous person, but for those who are lawless and rebellious, for

> the ungodly and sinners, for the unholy and profane, for those who kill their fathers or mothers, for murderers and immoral men and homosexuals and kidnappers and liars and perjurers, and whatever else is contrary to sound teaching.

The Greek word for "homosexuals" is *arsenokoitai,* which is best translated as "males who take other males to bed." Obviously, the word refers to those involved in homosexual behavior.

Each of the aforementioned Bible passages should be understood in the broader context of God's design for human sexuality. God's plan is found in His creation (Genesis 1–2). He created humans as male and female in His image and likeness (Genesis 1:27). Sex was intended to occur between a man and woman within God-ordained marriage. Sex outside of such marriage (premarital sex, extramarital sex, and homosexual sex) is sin.

Did Jesus remove God's condemnation of homosexuality?

One of the most frequent arguments used in support of the morality of homosexuality involves the person of Jesus Christ. Prohomosexual commentators point out that Jesus never said anything about homosexuality. They reason that if Jesus didn't explicitly forbid a behavior, then that behavior must no longer be immoral.

But let's consider just a few of the many immoral acts that Jesus did not explicitly address: these include incest, bestiality, pedophilia, and a long list of other sexual sins. His silence does not mean that these are now moral acts. He also did not address such issues as domestic abuse, environmental degradation, euthanasia, and other topics of concern to which we can apply a biblical perspective.

Jesus did indirectly address homosexuality when He talked about the destruction of the cities of Sodom and Gomorrah as an example of God's judgment (Matthew 10:15; Luke 10:12; 17:29). These two cities were known for their rampant homosexuality, so the reference to God's judgment of sexual sin should have let His listeners know how God felt about such sin.

Now, Jesus *did* address the issue of human sexuality (Matthew 19:4-5) when He spoke about divorce. He quoted from Genesis 1–2 to remind those around Him that God's plan was for a male and female to be united in marriage. And when Jesus referred to the Old Testament, He clearly taught that He was not abolishing "the Law or the Prophets" (Matthew 5:17). That would certainly include the moral laws about homosexuality.

Were David and Jonathan homosexual?

David and Jonathan provide perhaps the best example of male friendship in the Old Testament. Homosexuals say the two had a homosexual relationship. But the only way anyone can believe that their relationship was homosexual in nature is to believe that *any* love one man has for another is sexual.

Jonathan first meets David after David slays Goliath. First Samuel 18:1 says, "Now it came about when he had finished speaking to Saul, that the soul of Jonathan was knit to the soul of David, and Jonathan loved him as himself." The two men had a love for one another, but it was not a sexual love.

Those who want to believe that this love was sexual often raise one of two issues. First, the Bible records that they kissed (1 Samuel 20:41) when they parted after Jonathan warned David that his father, Saul, intended to harm David. There is nothing in the passage that indicates this kiss was sexual. And anyone who has traveled overseas recognizes that heterosexual men occasionally kiss one another. This was especially true in the ancient Near East.

Second, some point to the eulogy that David gave of Jonathan.

David was brokenhearted over the loss of his friend and says, "Your love to me was more wonderful than the love of women" (2 Samuel 1:26). But again, nothing here indicates that this was sexual love. David was saying that his committed love for and friendship with Jonathan was far superior to any erotic love he felt from his wives. The fact David had many wives and concubines shows that his problem was not homosexual temptation but rather heterosexual lust that could not be fulfilled (which is why he committed adultery with Bathsheba even though he already had many other women).

Is homosexuality the worst of all sins?

We live in a society that often ranks immoral behavior. People place lying and gossip on the lower rungs of the moral ladder and murder and pedophilia on the top rungs. Usually they do this to feel better about their wrong attitudes or behaviors by saying "Well, at least I've never murdered anyone."

Christians do this as well. We have our own hierarchy of sins. And there is some validity to this. After all, some sins are worthy of criminal punishment, while others are not. But in God's eyes, sin is sin. Jesus died for all sins, both great and small.

Nevertheless, in Christian circles, some view homosexuality as the worst of all sins. One reason for this belief is the way the Bible describes God's reaction to homosexual sin. The Bible calls homosexuality "an abomination" (Leviticus 18:22). The Hebrew word for "abomination" is *toeva,* and it is used not only to describe how God feels about homosexuality, but also about adultery and many other sins.

In Proverbs 6:16-19 is a list of seven other sins that God calls an abomination:

> There are six things which the LORD hates, yes, seven which are an abomination to Him: haughty eyes, a lying

tongue, and hands that shed innocent blood, a heart that devises wicked plans, feet that run rapidly to evil, a false witness who utters lies, and one who spreads strife among brothers.

Considering the many sins that God calls an abomination, homosexuality is merely one of them. Homosexuality is not "the unforgivable sin," and it is not worse than other sexual sins such as adultery. Also, the Bible frequently lists other sins right along with sexual sins:

> Now the deeds of the flesh are evident, which are: immorality, impurity, sensuality, idolatry, sorcery, enmities, strife, jealousy, outbursts of anger, disputes, dissensions, factions, envying, drunkenness, carousing, and things like these, of which I forewarn you, just as I have forewarned you, that those who practice such things will not inherit the kingdom of God (Galatians 5:19-21).

The Bible teaches that "there is none righteous, not even one" (Romans 3:10). "All have sinned and fall short of the glory of God" (Romans 3:23).

Does homosexuality involve deception?

Often when those involved in homosexuality are confronted by the biblical perspective on this sexual sin, they immediately reject it and often try to find a way to justify their attitudes and actions. Why is this?

It should not surprise us that sexual sins often involve a form of spiritual deception. This is true of premarital sex, extramarital sex, and homosexual sex. We should note that when Paul talks about God's perspective on sexual sins, he often uses the word *deceived*. He does this because he is aware of how the human mind can easily rationalize sexual sin. Consider the following passages:

Do not be deceived, God is not mocked; for whatever a man sows, this he will also reap. For the one who sows to his own flesh will from the flesh reap corruption, but the one who sows to the Spirit will from the Spirit reap eternal life (Galatians 6:7-8).

Do not be deceived; neither fornicators, nor idolaters, nor adulterers, nor effeminate, nor homosexuals, nor thieves, nor the covetous, nor drunkards, nor revilers, nor swindlers, will inherit the kingdom of God (1 Corinthians 6:9-10).

Let no one deceive you with empty words, for because of these things the wrath of God comes upon the sons of disobedience. Therefore do not be partakers with them (Ephesians 5:6-7).

We should be careful to make sure that we are not deceived by a culture that may try to conform us to its image and oppose the clear teaching of the Bible (Romans 12:1-2).

HOMOSEXUALITY AND THE CHURCH

Are homosexuality and Christianity compatible? While the answer from the Bible is no, the answer from many churches and denominations is yes. The prevalent and misleading theology of our day preaches tolerance and thus welcomes practicing homosexuals into the church and even into the pastorate.

What are some of the basic beliefs of the gay church? And how do they reconcile these beliefs with the Bible? These are important questions we should be able to answer as we interact with those who have adopted a progay gospel.

What can churches do to reach out to homosexuals? How do we deal with the inherent tension between our biblical convictions and our biblical compassion? And what can we do when someone says, "I'm gay"? Let's look for the answers in this chapter.

Where do churches and denominations stand on homosexuality?

Christian denominations vary greatly in their response to homosexuality. Liberal denominations and Christians tend to view homosexuality as a matter of rights and therefore ignore or reinterpret the key Bible passages concerning homosexuality. They see homosexual orientation as something innate, natural, and thus morally neutral.

Some denominations welcome people of all sexual orientations into their congregation and even allow their ministers to perform same-sex union ceremonies. Others permit those with a homosexual orientation into the clergy. One well-known example is Reverend Gene Robinson, who was confirmed in 2003 as the first openly gay bishop in the Episcopal Church's history.

While these denominations and churches usually portray themselves as open-minded and inclusive, their actions and affirmations are contrary to the Bible. Moreover, their preaching and doctrine are missing the fundamental aspects of the Christian life. Two Christian authors talk about what is missing in these churches:

> Absent are passionate calls to righteousness and to obedience to God's revealed will. Gone is the New Testament repugnance for sexual immorality and an alternative passion for purity. Gone is the vision for the chaste life of singleness as a lifestyle of dignity and delight. Gone is any sense of how our sexuality, and indeed our faith, can serve purposes beyond meeting our own needs. Absent is a vision for how our sexuality must be harnessed and channeled to serve higher ends. Absent is a cautious awareness of just how contaminated our lives are by the fall and by sin, and of how profound is our capacity for self-deception and desperate need for God's guidance in how to live our lives.[1]

Conservative denominations and Christians usually view human sexuality through the lens of Scripture and therefore see any sexual activity outside of God-ordained marriage as sinful. They generally see homosexual orientation as something chosen and changeable. They would not allow a homosexual to continue in his lifestyle or to serve as a minister.

What are the basic beliefs in a gay church?

The Metropolitan Community Church is the most prominent of the gay churches in America. Its founder, Troy Perry, is an openly homosexual ex-Baptist minister who lost his ministry license after the discovery and disclosure of his homosexuality. "Tens of thousands of so-called faithful 'Christian' homosexual men and women flock weekly to MCC-affiliated churches worldwide to be 'reaffirmed' with the message that God loves them and 'gay is OK.'"[2]

Troy Perry is highly regarded in homosexual circles. He has been an invited guest to the White House on many occasions, with three of those invitations from former president Bill Clinton. And in 1997, Clinton celebrated Perry as an "honoree" at a White House breakfast that recognized various national "spiritual leaders" in America.

According to Troy Perry and the material he and his fellow pastors have placed on the church's Web site, orthodox Christians have been misinterpreting the Bible in regard to homosexuality. Here is a summary of some of the Metropolitan Church's beliefs:[3]

- The Bible is full of errors that have resulted from being copied, recopied, and translated over and over again.

- Homosexuality is *not* a sin in God's eyes.

- References to homosexuality in the Bible actually refer to other things, and not homosexuality.

- Sodom and Gomorrah were not destroyed because of homosexuality, but because the people in those cities didn't feed the poor and needy.

- Jonathan and David were homosexual lovers, and the biblical story is one of hot, passionate gay romance, kissing, jealousy, and sex.

- Ruth and Naomi were lesbian lovers.

- There are numerous other possible gays and lesbians throughout the Bible who have been "kept in the closet" by homophobic Christians throughout the centuries.

- Jesus Christ actually "lived an alternative lifestyle" and the apostle John, "the disciple whom Jesus loved," could have been his gay male lover.

- According to eight other biblical references, Jesus possibly "loved" many other men as well.

- Jesus Christ wore a robe of purple to the cross (a color adopted by gays), a possible gay and lesbian connotation.

Are there different types of homosexuals?

It is a mistake to generalize about people, and that is certainly true about those who refer to themselves as homosexuals. But it is also important to understand where others are coming from when you engage them in conversation. A number of Christian authors have said there are basically three different groups of homosexuals: repentant, moderate, and militant.[4]

Repentant—People in this category are often caught between a rock and a hard place. They see the gay community embracing gay sex, but must also deal with the traditional message of the church and Western culture. So they hear and struggle between two messages. One is that they should embrace their homosexuality. The other is that they should reject their feelings because homosexual behavior is sinful.

Those who fall into this category do so for several reasons. Some may have been raised in the church and fallen away from their spiritual commitment. Others may have tried to make sense of their feelings and temptations and then decided to reject the church and try embracing the gay community. Still others may be living a divided life: going to church but still engaging in the gay lifestyle.

The key issue here is holiness. Various Christian ministries to homosexuals will often say that "the opposite of homosexuality is not heterosexuality, it's holiness." A truly repentant homosexual will no doubt desire personal holiness. The "goal is to lay down the lesser love of homosexuality and embrace the greater love of Christ's atonement." [5]

One danger for repentant homosexuals is the tendency for churches to put them in front of crowds to give their testimony too early. Obviously they have a story to tell, but we are warned in 1 Timothy 3:6 to make sure that we do not raise up recent converts too early lest they become conceited and their testimony suffers.

Moderate—People in this category may not agree with the traditional biblical interpretation of homosexuality, but aren't necessarily antagonistic toward that interpretation either. They have developed a "live and let live" approach to life. Some may accept most of the gay agenda. Others may actually "challenge the gay establishment's groupthink regarding gay activism. Many are also mortified by what the militant gay activist community proposes on behalf of everyone else in the gay community."[6]

It is best to meet someone in this category on common-ground issues. If you are willing to listen and engage in a civil discussion, both of you can express your point of view and be heard. This can help build a basis for sharing and friendship.

Militant—People in this category frequently participate in gay pride parades and protests against individuals and churches. They are working not only to get everyone in society to tolerate their actions and agenda, but they want society to approve of them as well through mandates, policies, and legal action.

It is usually very difficult to maintain civil discourse with people in this group. But it is still important to maintain civility even when a militant person does not do so. The Bible teaches that a gentle answer turns away wrath (Proverbs 15:1). But that does not mean that a militant person will be content with a gracious, well-reasoned response. Nevertheless, our response as Christians should be loving and truthful regardless of how we're treated.

What can churches do to reach out to homosexuals?

One of the biggest challenges for churches and individual Christians who reach out to homosexuals is keeping two principles in proper tension: biblical convictions and biblical compassion. Often it is difficult to keep truth and love in a proper dynamic tension, but that is what we must do if we are to faithfully follow the Bible's commands to us.

In recent decades, churches have responded to homosexuals in different ways.[7] There is the permissive church, which focuses mainly on expressing compassion and fails to understand the need for telling the truth about moral issues. There is the rebellious church that has openly gay members and celebrates their sexuality. While the permissive church tends to ignore biblical teaching, the rebellious church openly defies biblical commands.

On the other extreme is the judgmental church that tends to err on the side of truth and ignore biblical compassion. There is also the uncommitted church that neither helps homosexuals out of their sin nor teaches a biblical message that would convict them of their sin. And there is the ignorant church that simply does not know what God's Word teaches regarding homosexuality.

The ideal goal is for a church to believe what God's Word says and thus understand the need to confront sin, and also be willing to reach out to those caught in sinful behavior. These leaders and members will be committed to reaching out to homosexuals in grace, truth, and love.

Here are four key principles that the church and Christian individual should follow:

1. *The church must lovingly speak out against sexual sin.* The Bible is God's unchanging Word and should not be compromised to suit changing cultural circumstances. All sexual sin, including homosexuality, is contrary to the Bible. And we must consistently speak out against sexual immorality (1 Corinthians 6:18) and sexual sins (Ephesians 5:3), especially within the church.

Sometimes the church must do more than just speak out against sin; it must deal with persistent sexual sin within the congregation. Sexual sin is not just a personal matter, but a problem that the church must address. The Bible teaches that we must confront individuals involved in any kind of sin (Matthew 18:15-20), and that ongoing, unrepentant sin can be cause for excommunication (1 Corinthians 5:1-13). Enforcing these biblical standards is for the good of the church body (1 Corinthians 5:6). The church cannot afford to minimize flagrant sexual sin when it occurs within the congregation. And confrontation should always be done with gentleness in an attempt to restore the sinner to righteousness (Galatians 6:1).

2. *The church should lovingly welcome those who struggle with homosexual temptations.* We should reject homophobia and the condemnation of people who struggle with homosexual temptation. We should create a loving and caring environment where people can openly discuss their feelings without shame or rejection.

3. *The church should dedicate itself to meeting the emotional and*

spiritual needs of those who struggle with homosexuality. The church should be a place that provides supportive care and authentic relationships within the body of Christ. This can take place within the whole church body as well as through a small group context so that believers may be strengthened in their faith toward spiritual maturity.

4. *The church should reach out to homosexuals in the community.* The church should have a positive testimony in the community because those in the homosexual community usually view the church as an enemy. They see it as a place of judgmental people who would never welcome them or consider ministering to them. Jesus responded with love to sinners in His midst. In Luke 19:10, Jesus said, "The Son of Man has come to seek and to save that which was lost."

How should I respond when someone says, "I'm gay"?

Many good articles and brochures have been written that answer this question. The following is a summary of some key points in a brochure ("When Someone In Your Congregation Says 'I'm Gay'") that provides a list of things of remember and things to avoid.[8]

1. *Remember that no one is born gay, and no one chooses to be gay.* As we already discussed in chapter 5, human sexuality is complex. It is rarely helpful to spend time trying to determine the origin or cause of a person's sexual temptations. That might be helpful for a counselor, but not for a lay Christian.

Because of past emotional brokenness in relation to families or friends, some people will experience emotional needs that they try to meet in ungodly ways. These people may be uncomfortable with their own gender and may act upon their feelings and temptations in ways that violate biblical commands.

2. *Remember that change is possible.* The testimony of hundreds

of former homosexuals is proof that change is possible. So are the various studies that document these same behavioral changes. And the Bible also teaches that change is possible. Paul, when he wrote to former homosexuals in the Corinthian church, noted that "such were some of you" (1 Corinthians 6:11).

3. *Remember that homosexuality grows out of broken relationships.* This also means that homosexuality can be healed in healthy relationships, especially healthy same-sex relationships. That is why it's essential for homosexuals who are struggling with their feelings to be actively involved in the church. The church can and should be a place where they can find healthy, God-honoring friendships.

4. *Speak the truth in love.* Choose to love sinners even as you disagree with their sinful behavior. People don't change when they are rejected and condemned. They change when they hear the truth spoken with love. That's what draws them toward Christianity.

5. *Share Christ with them.* Some homosexuals feel as though they have committed the unpardonable sin. They've heard and felt condemnation from people inside and outside the church. They believe they are going to hell and there is no hope for them. They need to know the truth of 1 John 1:9: "If we confess our sins, He is faithful and righteous to forgive us our sins and to cleanse us from all unrighteousness."

6. *Pastors need to develop a shepherding role.* Pastors are men in authority. Therefore, most strugglers (men and women) are intimidated by them. So pastors need to understand this dynamic in order to effectively minister. For example, they should respect the fragility of the person struggling with homosexuality. In their relationship, pastors should be tender and gentle. Homosexuals really need "good shepherds" and encouragers.

7. *Guard and protect the relationship.* Most who struggle with

homosexuality have weak or broken boundaries. Their neediness may cause them to lapse into emotionally dependent relationships with everyone who gets close to them. Counsel at your office only during regular business hours so others can be aware of your activities.

8. *Don't back down.* If someone comes with an agenda and demands acceptance of his sexual sin, don't let him bully you. Showing biblical compassion toward sinners does not mean we have to compromise our biblical convictions. As we learned in the chapter titled "Homosexuality and the Bible," there are many verses that condemn homosexual behavior.

9. *Don't panic.* You don't have to have all the answers. In addition to this book, there are many others listed in the bibliography on page 131 as well as many good Web sites that can provide you with answers to the questions people ask you about homosexuality.

10. *Don't make false assumptions or accusations.* Don't assume a homosexual is militant in his or her stance. Don't assume he is HIV positive. Even if he is, AIDS is not transmitted by casual contact. The members of your congregation are safe.

11. *Don't shut down pastorally or emotionally.* Remember that the homosexual person has probably known a lifetime of rejection. He or she needs to know that a follower of Christ will give grace. Be a positive person and encourage him or her toward righteousness.

12. *Don't pass judgment.* All have sinned and fall short of the glory of God (Romans 3:23). As Billy Graham has said, "Don't take credit for not falling into a temptation that never tempted you in the first place."

SAME-SEX MARRIAGE AND POLITICS

FOR THOUSANDS OF YEARS, societies have defined marriage in essentially the same way. The reasons for this include experience, tradition, social custom, legal precedent, and religious teaching. Marriage is a unique relationship in which a man and a woman join together for the purpose of establishing a family.

The recognition of marriage as an institution predates the formal legal recognition provided by governments today. But in recent years many gay activists have wanted to redefine the legal definition of marriage to include same-sex marriages. This has led to a response from various groups to formally define marriage through state and federal constitutional amendments.

Why has same-sex marriage become an issue?

The current attempts to redefine marriage go back more than a decade. In 1993, the Supreme Court of Hawaii ruled that the state's existing marriage statute was a form of "sex discrimination" that could only be justified by a compelling state interest.[1] Three years later, a trial court in that same state ruled that the state marriage law was in violation of the constitution of Hawaii.[2] The people of Hawaii responded by amending their state constitution so that the legislature could reserve marriage for opposite-sex couples. Then the legislature passed the Marriage Protection Act, which defined marriage as the union between one man and one woman.

In 1996, the U.S. Congress passed the federal Defense of Marriage Act (DOMA), which was signed into law by then-President Bill Clinton. It defined marriage "for all purposes of federal law" as the union of one man and one woman. It also clarified the effect portion of the "full faith and credit clause" of the U.S. Constitution so that states would not be required to recognize same-sex marriages or civil unions in other states.[4]

> "Today's results prove that certain fundamental issues should not be left up to a majority vote."
>
> —Then-ACLU executive director **Ira Glasser**, after the citizens of Alaska passed a constitutional amendment barring same-sex marriage in 1998.[3]

Over the next two years, cases in California, Florida, and New York tried unsuccessfully to establish the recognition of same-sex marriages. Then in 1998, a superior court judge in Alaska ruled the Alaska marriage statute unconstitutional because "the choice of a life partner is personal, intimate, and subject to the protection of the right to privacy."[5] Voters in Alaska responded by passing a constitutional amendment defining marriage as a union between one man and one woman.

In 1999, the Supreme Court of Vermont ruled that the legislature must extend the benefits enjoyed by heterosexual married couples to same-sex couples.[6] In 2003, the U.S. Supreme Court ruled in *Lawrence v. Texas* that state laws against homosexual sodomy were unconstitutional.[7] The majority argued that intimate consensual sexual conduct was protected by due process under the Fourteenth Amendment. Their 6-3 ruling not only contradicted the court's 1986 ruling in *Bowers v. Hardwick,* but it set the foundation for a later ruling (in Massachusetts) that legalized same-sex marriage. The high court held that homosexuals have the right to "seek autonomy" in their relationships and cited "personal decisions relating to marriage."

In November 2003, four judges on the Massachusetts Supreme Judicial Court used these phrases to justify their ruling that same-sex marriages should be allowed in Massachusetts. The court gave the legislature 180 days "to take such action as it may deem appropriate" in order to implement their decision.[8]

It is important to remember that this decision was *not* put to a vote. It was the decision of four judges in Massachusetts. At the time, surveys showed that 72 percent of Americans said they opposed same-sex marriage. There were 38 states that had passed a Defense of Marriage Act (DOMA) that defined marriage as a union between one man and one woman, and many others states had passed or were in the process of passing constitutional amendments defining marriage as a union between one man and one woman.

When the Massachusetts legislature met in early 2004, the members asked the court if civil unions would be a sufficient mechanism to implement the decision. The Massachusetts judges ruled in February 2004 that civil unions were not sufficient.[9] They ordered that same-sex marriage licenses must be issued starting in May. Nothing less than same-sex marriage was allowed.

During this same period of time, a number of mayors in various cities began to issue marriage licenses to same-sex couples. These cities included San Francisco, California; Sandoval County, New Mexico; New Paltz, New York; and Multnomah County, Oregon. Eventually judges ruled these marriage licenses invalid, but the publicity surrounding the controversy helped build momentum toward the issuing of valid same-sex marriage licenses in Massachusetts.

Back in 2004, the Massachusetts legislature had begun the process of amending the Constitution of Massachusetts to define marriage as a union between one man and one woman. But the Massachusetts Supreme Judicial Court was unmoved by these actions. And so on May 17, 2004, the first legal same-sex marriage licenses were issued in Massachusetts.

The time from the U.S. Supreme Court decision in *Lawrence v. Texas* to the issuing of the first same-sex marriage licenses in Massachusetts was less than a year. There is some evidence to suggest this was part of a larger strategy. In the summer of 2003, Kevin Cathcart (executive director of the homosexual advocacy group Lambda Legal) outlined that very strategy. At the time he said, "We need a state court victory [that would allow same-sex marriage] before we can see any action on the federal level."[11] And it may be more than coincidence that the Massachusetts Supreme Judicial Court gave him that victory in November in the case of *Goodridge v. Massachusetts*.

Since the decision in Massachusetts, there has been a flurry of activity elsewhere at the state level to pass marriage amendments that would define marriage as a union between one man and one woman. More than half of the states have passed such amendments, often with more than 70 to 80 percent of the vote.

"Marriage is at the center of the family, and the family is the basis of society itself. The government's interest in the marriage bond, and the reason it treats heterosexual unions in a manner unlike all other relationships, is closely related to the welfare of children. Government registers and endorses marriage between a man and a woman in order to ensure a stable environment for the raising and nurturing of children."[10]

—Senator Sam Brownback
(R–Kansas)

All but one of these state marriage amendments passed the first time they were submitted to the voters.

Why do we need an amendment when we already have DOMA?

The federal government already passed the Defense of Marriage Act (DOMA) in 1996. Soon after, many states followed suit. Although many believe that DOMA should protect states, Glen Lavy (Alliance Defense Fund) argues that courts may not be stopped by these laws. He acknowledges that a challenge to DOMA "cannot succeed based on legal precedent." But we now live in a world "when courts say that they can redefine terms."[13]

Before DOMA was signed into law, Lambda Legal argued that it was unconstitutional. The organization argued back in 1996 that the full faith and credit clause of the U.S. Constitution was "intended to promote national unity" and assure that people "can move throughout the country without being stripped of their legal rights."

Michael Ferris (president of Patrick Henry College) told a Senate subcommittee that an increasing number of law review periodicals argue that DOMA is unconstitutional. "It is the dominant view, and I can tell you," he said, "that what's the dominant view in the law reviews today will be the dominant view of the courts in a generation."[14]

> "Fundamental human rights should never be put up for a popular vote. We'll win some states and we'll lose some states, but eventually the Supreme Court is going to look at the Bill of Rights and isn't going to give a damn what's in any of these state constitutions."[12]
>
> **—Matt Foreman,**
> executive director of National Gay and Lesbian Task Force

This is why many have proposed that a Marriage Protection Amendment (formerly called the Federal Marriage Amendment) be adopted by Congress and submitted to the states for ratification. The original amendment was written by the Alliance for Marriage (an organization founded by Matt Daniels). It was drafted in the spring and summer of 2001 with the help of former Supreme Court nominee Robert Bork and professor Robert George of Princeton University.[15]

The amendment was originally proposed by Representative Marilyn Musgrave (R–Colorado) in 2002. It reads,

> Marriage in the United States of America shall consist only of the union of a man and a woman. Neither this constitution or the constitution of any state, nor state or federal law, shall be construed to require that marital status or the legal incidents thereof be conferred upon unmarried couples or groups.

How will the legalization of same-sex marriage affect the church?

It appears that churches and pastors will be affected by the legalization of same-sex marriage even though gay activists deny it. Some gay activists make a distinction between civil marriage and religious marriage. One prohomosexual Web site puts it this way: "Religious institutions will never be forced to bless relationships with which they disagree, just as today religious institutions can refuse to marry couples of different faiths or individuals who have been divorced."[16]

While that might be true in the short term, Princeton professor Robert P. George believes that conflicts could arise later on. He points out that according to gay activists, preventing same-sex marriage constitutes bigotry. He argues that "if the belief in traditional marriage is a form of bigotry, then people who hold that belief and act on it in the religious sphere are likely to be treated the way racial bigots are treated when they act on racial bigotry in the religious sphere."[17]

Ministers probably won't be forced to perform a gay wedding. But it is possible that their churches could lose their tax-exempt status. The IRS pulled the tax-exempt status of Bob Jones University because of its racial policies. The university sued, claiming that its religious liberties had been violated. The U.S. Supreme Court, however, sided with the IRS. This case might provide a precedent if same-sex marriage is treated as a civil right.

"That alien mindset is what we should really be worried about… This mindset is a point of view that does not simply seek permission to engage in certain kinds of behavior. It seeks instead to ensure that everyone else in society also engages in that same behavior, or at least gives it tacit approval… Rather than being surprised when that happens, we should be surprised if it does not happen just that way. Nor is it unthinkable in such a climate that courts will rule soon that *World* magazine, and other organizations like us, will be required to hire employees—including editorial writers—who are ardent proponents of same-sex marriage, and, of course, who have already entered such relationships."[18]

—**Joel Belz,** founder and publisher of *World* magazine

Harvard University law professor Mary Ann Glendon, writing in the *Wall Street Journal,* put it this way:

> Gay-marriage proponents use the language of openness, tolerance and diversity, yet one foreseeable effect of their success will be to usher in an era of intolerance and

discrimination the likes of which we have rarely seen before. Every person and every religion that disagrees will be labeled as bigoted and openly discriminated against. The ax will fall most heavily on religious persons and groups that don't go along. Religious institutions will be hit with lawsuits if they refuse to compromise their principles.[19]

How will the legalization of same-sex marriage affect society?

The legalization of same-sex marriage will affect not only the church, but also society at large. The following are just a few ways in which various segments of society will be affected:

Freedom of association—If same-sex marriage becomes legal, then a natural next step will be to ban discrimination in hiring based upon sexual orientation. Churches, synagogues, religious schools, and faith-based organizations would not be allowed to refuse to hire someone who was a practicing homosexual.

Freedom of speech—Legalizing same-sex marriage will no doubt impact a person's ability to address the moral aspect of homosexuality. Some of the examples of the growing opposition to a biblical perspective on homosexuality demonstrate how this is already happening. Even more opposition is likely against individuals and organizations that uphold traditional marriage and verbalize moral and religious objections to homosexuality. They will be stigmatized and marginalized by society in general.

Public school curriculum—As seen in the chapter "Homosexuality and the Schools," within many school districts, homosexuality is already being taught as merely an alternative lifestyle. Legalizing same-sex marriage will further establish homosexuality in public school curriculum. Not only will students be taught about homosexuality, but they will probably be instructed that opposition to homosexuality is a vestige of America's dark past of discrimination (similar to racial discrimination). Homosexual marriage will be presented as equal to heterosexual marriage.

"They [advocates of polyandry] have all sorts of arrangements, you know, two women and three men, any kind of a combination, a kind of group marriage. And polyamorists (individuals who support multi-partner relationships and families) have already had a law case arguing that their marriages should be recognized."[20]

—**Stanley Kurtz,** Hoover Institution

Social services—The legalization of same-sex marriage in Massachusetts has already provided an illustration of the impact such an action can have on various social services. Consider the case of Catholic Charities of Boston. On March 10, 2006, the organization announced that it was being forced to shut down their adoption services because of governmental regulations. This highly regarded adoption agency had to shut its doors because it could not, in good conscience, follow the government's demands that they place children with homosexual couples.

Catholic teaching considers gay adoptions as "gravely immoral." So the Boston archdiocese sought a religious exemption from the governmental requirement that adoption agencies place children in homes of parents who have different sexual orientations. Even though Catholic Charities had been providing excellent service, they were denied a waiver from the government. They were forced to end their services to the community, some of which were vital. One columnist at the time noted that "Catholic Charities excels at arranging adoptions for children in foster care, particularly those who are older or handicapped."[21]

Let's be clear: Catholic Charities was *not* trying to change the government regulations. And Catholic Charities was *not* trying to prevent homosexual couples from adoption. In fact, the agency would routinely refer gay couples to other adoption agencies that would be willing to facilitate their adoption of a child.

All Catholic Charities was asking is that they be permitted to do what they had been doing for nearly a century: placing children in homes they felt were suitable. If homosexual couples wanted to adopt a child, they would let other agencies provide those services for them. All the government needed to do was grant the organization's request for a conscience clause and leave the task of gay adoptions to other agencies that would be more than willing to provide those services.

Granting Catholic Charities a waiver would not have prevented children from being placed with homosexual couples. Other agencies would still be free to help such couples. By contrast, when the government drove Catholic Charities out of business, they guaranteed that the agency would never again be able to help place children in loving homes.

Do we need the Employment Non-Discrimination Act?

One legislative act that would extend governmental oversight and legal pressure against companies is the Employment Non-Discrimination Act (known as ENDA). This legislation nearly passed in the U.S. Senate and will continually be reintroduced into Congress by gay advocacy groups. Quite simply, this act would have added the category of sexual orientation to the 1964 Civil Rights Act.

There is some reason to question whether homosexuals even qualify as an oppressed class of people. One study released by Simmons Research found that the average income of homosexual households was $85,000, which is more than twice the national average.[22] Another study done at Syracuse University found that the median income for homosexual couples was $65,000, which is nearly 60 percent higher than the national median of $40,800.[23]

These are not the income statistics of an oppressed class. Moreover, one leader of the homosexual organization the Log Cabin Republicans questioned the need for ENDA. He said, "I can tell you anecdotally that as I travel all over the country, I almost never hear from anyone who was fired because they were gay."[24] It appears the major justification for ENDA is to provide the government with one more tool to intimidate and punish individuals and organizations that disagree with the gay agenda.

ANSWERING THE ARGUMENTS FOR SAME-SEX MARRIAGE

THE PROMOTION OF HOMOSEXUALITY in the public arena has led to a robust debate about the pros and cons of legalizing same-sex marriage. Many of the clichés and arguments for same-sex marriage need to be discussed and answered. At the forefront is the argument for tolerance in society. How should Christians respond to this demand for tolerance?

Same-sex marriage is also promoted as a second civil rights movement. Don't homosexuals deserve equal rights when it comes to marriage? And isn't an objection to homosexual marriage much like an objection to interracial marriage?

Proponents of same-sex marriage argue that legalizing it won't affect society. And when confronted with concerns, they ask how permitting same-sex marriage could possibly hurt traditional marriage. But are these assertions true?

Shouldn't we be tolerant of other lifestyles?

We used to live in a society where the highest value was a word with a capital T—the word *Truth*. Today we live in a society that has switched that value for another value that also begins with a capital T: *Tolerance.*

Should we be tolerant of other people and their lifestyles? The answer to that depends upon the definition of *tolerance.* If by tolerance someone means we should be civil to other people, then the answer is a resounding yes. In fact, civility should be the hallmark of Christians toward everyone. Jesus expressed the goal of civility when He taught, "You shall love your neighbor as yourself" (Matthew 22:39).

Civility also includes being gracious even in the midst of disagreement or hostility. Other people may disagree with us, and we are free to disagree with them. But we should disagree in a way that shows grace. Often a gentle response can change the tone of a difficult discussion. Proverbs 15:1 reminds us that "a gentle answer turns away wrath."

Civility also requires humility. A civil person acknowledges that he or she does not possess all wisdom and knowledge. Therefore, we should listen to others and consider the possibility that they might be right and that we might be wrong. Philippians 2:3 says, "Do nothing from selfishness or empty conceit, but with humility of mind let each of you regard one another as more important than himself."

If, however, the definition of tolerance includes affirmation and acceptance of sinful behavior, Christians cannot agree. They can take comfort in knowing that even the apostle Paul was falsely accused of intolerance (Acts 21:27-29)—way back in the first century.

Those who reject attempts to redefine marriage by legalizing same-sex marriage do so out of personal convictions. And those who believe that homosexuality is sinful believe so out of biblical convictions. These convictions are based upon a biblical worldview. Critics who accuse Christians of being prejudiced or bigoted are really rejecting a proper biblical perspective that has been held by Christians for millennia. Also in favor of traditional marriages is the fact these marriages have historically proven the most effective. There are some, however, who want to throw out biblical convictions and historical experience in lieu of a social experiment with same-sex marriage.

There is also an important distinction we should make between judging a person and judging his or her sinful behavior. Some have said that the most frequently quoted Bible verse is no longer John 3:16 but Matthew 7:1, where Jesus said, "Do not judge, or you too will be judged." People misuse this verse to say you should not judge anything another person does.

The context of this verse is important. It seems that Jesus was condemning a critical or judgmental spirit. Jesus was *not* saying that people should not make judgments. A few verses later, Jesus calls certain people "pigs" and "dogs" (Matthew 7:6). He even calls some "wolves in sheep's clothing" (Matthew 7:15). There are many passages in the Bible that admonish us to use sound judgment and discernment (for example, 1 Kings 3:9; Proverbs 15:14; Philippians 1:9-10).

The Bible says Jesus was "full of grace and truth" (John 1:14) and that He provides a model we should follow. We should exhibit both biblical compassion and biblical convictions when addressing the issues of homosexuality and same-sex marriage.

Don't homosexuals deserve equal rights?

Every person in our society deserves equal rights. But redefining marriage is not about equal rights—rather, it's about adding special rights to our laws and Constitution. Currently we all have the same right to marry a person of the opposite sex who is of a certain age and background. We don't give people the right to marry their siblings or a young child. As a society, we have placed certain limits on marriage, but we still give everyone the equal right to marry under those specified conditions.

When we redefine marriage, however, all sorts of new relationships will also vie for social acceptance. Already the legalization of same-sex marriage in one state has resulted in a call to legalize polygamy. Some gay activists are calling for the legalization of polyamory (multiple sexual relationships with multiple partners).

We should also realize that the government does not prohibit homosexuals from engaging in their behavior or even having a partner. All the government has said so far is that it is not going to redefine marriage to include same-sex relationships. And when citizens of America have been given the opportunity to vote on a constitutional amendment about the definition of marriage, they have overwhelmingly approved of the traditional definition.

> "Same-sex marriage is not about civil rights. It's about validation and social respect. It is a radical attempt at civil engineering using government muscle to strong-arm people into accommodating a lifestyle many find deeply offensive, contrary to nature, socially destructive, and morally repugnant."[1]
>
> —**Greg Koukl,** president, Stand to Reason

As we have already noted, the push for same-sex marriage has been more about respect and acceptance than it has been about rights. If the government legally validates gay marriage, then that places the government's "seal of approval" on homosexuality.

Often when gay activists are calling for equal rights, they are really asking for special benefits. Homosexuals have the same right to marry as heterosexuals. They have the right to marry a qualified person (age, marital status) of the opposite sex. Homosexuals and heterosexuals cannot marry someone of the same sex, someone who is too young, someone who is already married, etc.

But gay activists argue that because they cannot marry someone of the same sex, they lose out on certain benefits. But that is not a justification for redefining marriage. It may be a justification for reconsidering the benefits we provide as a society, but it isn't a justification for changing the definition of marriage.

Consider the issue of taxation. For the sake of discussion, let's assume that homosexual couples are subject to a different rate of taxation than heterosexual couples. We as a society can decide what an appropriate rate of taxation might be. People who are married and people who are single have different rates of taxation. People who make more money have a different rate of taxation than those who make less. If we need to change the rate of taxation for a homosexual couple, then let's change the rate of taxation. But we don't need to change the definition of marriage as well.

> " 'Gay citizens'" already have the same right to marry as anyone else—subject to the same restrictions. No one may marry a close blood relative, a child, a person who is already married, or a person of the same sex. However much those restrictions may disappoint the incestuous, pedophiles, polygamists, and homosexuals, the issue is not discrimination. It is the nature of marriage itself."[2]
>
> —**Peter Sprigg**, vice president for policy, Family Research Council

A number of years ago, members of Congress pointed out there was a marriage penalty in the tax code. Those who were married were paying more in taxes than if they were single and living together. Congress changed the tax code; it didn't need to change the definition of marriage.

Another issue is that of hospital visitation rights. Gay activists argue that government needs to grant same-sex marriage rights to homosexuals so they will have visitation rights. But this may be an argument for changing the laws concerning visitation rather than the laws concerning marriage.

Also, are visitation rights really a problem? In this day of major corporations and governmental entities granting domestic partnership rights, this hasn't really been a problem. Many of my radio talk show guests have said they are unaware of any hospital that doesn't allow a homosexual partner visitation rights. And if such a case were brought to light, public pressure would likely force the hospital to change its policy.

Isn't homosexual marriage like interracial marriage?

When objections are raised against legalizing same-sex marriage, proponents argued that the same concerns were voiced about interracial marriage. For years gay activists have tried to hitch their caboose to the civil rights train. While many in the African-American community have found this comparison offensive, the tactic is still used on a fairly regular basis.

There are significant differences between interracial marriage and same-sex marriage. First, the removal of certain state laws banning interracial marriage did not call for a *redefinition* of marriage, but rather, an *affirmation* of marriage. Traditional marriage is not about equal rights but about establishing norms for sexual relationships within society. It is right that we ban discrimination based on race because race is an immutable characteristic that each person has from the moment of conception. Also, the word *race* appears in the U.S. Constitution.

By contrast, homosexual *behavior* is not an immutable characteristic. As many people have pointed out, there are no former African-Americans or former Asian-Americans. But there are hundreds of people who have left homosexuality.[3]

Interracial marriage and same-sex marriage differ from one another at the most fundamental level. The genetic difference between various races is insignificant biologically. A recent study of the human genetic material of different races concluded that the DNA of any two people in the world will differ by just two-tenths of 1 percent.[4] And of this variation, only 6 percent can be linked to racial categories. The remaining 94 percent is "within race" variation. And the moral difference between the races is also insignificant for the Bible teaches that God has made all of us from "one blood" (Acts 17:26 KJV).

So while race and ethnicity are insignificant to marriage, gender is not. There is a profound biological difference between a man and a woman. Marriage has always been defined as a bond between a man and a woman.

The Supreme Court case *Loving v. Virginia* struck down state laws prohibiting interracial marriage by arguing that marriage is one of the "basic civil rights of man."[5] The Supreme Court of Minnesota later ruled in *Baker v. Nelson* that race and homosexual behavior are not analogous. The court said,

> *Loving* does indicate that not all state restrictions upon the right to marriage are beyond reach of the Fourteenth Amendment. But in commonsense and in a constitutional sense, there is a clear distinction between a marital restriction based on race and one based on the fundamental difference in sex.[6]

To legalize same-sex marriage is to change the very nature and definition of marriage. And there is good reason to believe that is exactly what gay activists want. Michelangelo Signorile is a leading voice in the homosexual community. He explained in *Out* magazine the real goal in legalizing same-sex marriage:

> The trick is, gay leaders and pundits must stop watering the issue down—"this is simply about equality for gay

couples"—and offer same-sex marriage for what it is: an opportunity to reconstruct a traditionally homophobic institution by bringing it to our more equitable queer value system…a chance to wholly transform the definition of family in American culture…Our gay leaders must acknowledge that gay marriage is just as *radical* and *transformative* as the religious Right contends it is.[7]

Later in the article he goes on to admit that the idea of the "freedom to marry" was actually a suggestion from a Los Angeles public relations firm. They thought this strategy would be successful because it would play well in the heterosexual world.

How does same-sex marriage hurt traditional marriage?

One of the arguments against the legalization of same-sex marriage is that it will have an adverse effect on traditional marriage. Proponents of same-sex marriage argue otherwise. They ask, "How can my marriage to someone of the same sex have any impact at all on your heterosexual marriage?" Who's right? Let's consider the following:

First, when the state sanctions gay marriage, it sends a signal of legitimacy throughout the culture. Eventually marriage becomes nothing more than sexual partnership, and the sanctity of marriage and all that goes with it is lost.

Columnist Jeff Jacoby put it this way:

The adoption of same-sex marriage would topple a long-standing system of shared values. It would change assumptions and expectations by which society has long operated—that men and women are not interchangeable, and that the central reason for marriage is to provide children with mothers and fathers in a safe and loving environment.[8]

If same-sex marriage were legalized, subsequent generations would be confused about sexual identity. Ultimately, they would come to believe that there is fundamentally no difference between heterosexual and homosexual marriages. The law is a teacher of values, and the legalization of same-sex marriage would send a signal that a homosexual marriage is the same as a heterosexual one. Jacoby argues,

> My foreboding is that a generation after same-sex marriage is legalized, families will be even less stable than they are today, the divorce rate will be even higher and children will be even less safe. To express such a dire warning is to be labeled an alarmist, a reactionary, a bigot and worse…But it is not bigotry to learn from history, or to point out that some institutions have stood the test of time because they are the only ones that can stand the test of time.[9]

In places where same-sex marriage has been legalized, the incidences of cohabitation among the general population increases. This is not theory but sociological fact. Essentially, Europe has been engaged in a social experiment with same-sex marriage for decades.

Stanley Kurtz has written numerous articles documenting the impact of same-sex marriage on traditional marriage in Scandinavian countries. When the governments of Sweden and Norway permitted same-sex marriage, those countries experienced a trend *away* from marriage. According to Kurtz, "Marriage is slowly dying in Scandinavia." A majority of children in Sweden and Norway are born out of wedlock, and 60 percent of firstborn children in Denmark have unmarried parents.[10] Kurtz has also documented that marriage is in decline in the Netherlands.[11]

Second, the legalization of same-sex marriage would completely redefine marriage to the point of introducing a variety of other kinds of marital relationships. Already we are seeing court cases that are attempting to legalize polygamy. The most prominent case involved Utah polygamist Tom Green. He and his lawyer attempted to use the U.S. Supreme Court decision in *Lawrence v. Texas* as a legal foundation for his marriage to multiple wives.[12] It is interesting to note that when the Supreme Court rendered its decision in the *Lawrence* case, Justice Antonin Scalia warned that the decision could lead to the legalization of same-sex marriage and the redefinition of marriage.[13]

Once you redefine marriage so that it is no longer defined as a union between one man and one woman, almost any combination of partners can be considered. That would not only include one man and five women, but many other arrangements. A number of commentators and activists have talked about the possibility of polyamorous relationships that would include all sorts of combinations of men and women.

Traditional marriage rests on the foundation of biblical teaching as well as cultural tradition. Theology, legal precedent, and historical experience all support the traditional definition of marriage. Once you begin to redefine marriage, any sexual relationship can be called a marriage—to the detriment of family and society.

Third, the redefinition of marriage will ultimately destroy marriage as we know it. For many gay activists, the goal is not to simply permit same-sex marriages, but to destroy the institution of marriage.

In 1972, the National Coalition of Gay Organizations demanded "the repeal of all legislative provisions that restrict the sex or number of persons entering into a marriage unit; and the extension of legal benefits to all persons who cohabit regardless of sex or numbers."[14]

Clearly the goal of that demand was to extend all the benefits of marriage to *all* people and thus essentially eliminate the institution of marriage. And once marriage is eliminated or even minimized, couples would merely live together and not be bound to each other in the way they currently are under marriage laws.

Stanley Kurtz believes that once same-sex marriage is legalized, "marriage will be transformed into a variety of relationship contracts, linking two, three or more individuals (however weakly or temporarily) in every conceivable combination of male and female."[15]

No wonder there are some who are suggesting that the government get out of the marriage license business. Columnist Michael Kinsley wrote a column entitled, "Abolish Marriage: Get the Government Out of Our Bedrooms." He argued that the

> solution is to end the institution of marriage, or rather, the solution is to end the government monopoly on marriage. And yes, if three people want to get married, or one person wants to marry herself and someone else wants to conduct a ceremony and declare them married, let 'em.[16]

Kinsley believes that if government gets out of the marriage business, then all the disputes about gay marriage will end. History and current social experiences in other countries prove otherwise.

Finally, there is good reason to believe that homosexual marriages *will*, in fact, be different than heterosexual marriages, and ultimately they will influence the attitudes of those in traditional marriages. Homosexual commentator Andrew Sullivan has even predicted that gay couples would essentially change the way heterosexual couples view the institution of marriage. He cited "the need for extra-marital outlets" in same-sex marriages, which might cause heterosexuals to consider marriage an "open contract" that would allow both husband and wife to have additional sexual partners.[17]

That is exactly what is reported in one article that appeared in *New York* magazine. The article begins with the assumption that "for much of human history, monogamy (or, at least, presumed monogamy) has been the default setting for long-term love." It then tells the story of a heterosexual husband who desired an "open" marriage relationship after hearing about his gay friend's relationship. The article noted, "Many straight couples struggling with (monogamy) issues look to gay male friends, for whom a more fluid notion of commitment is practically the norm."[18]

In chapter 2, we reviewed a study in the Netherlands that found that gay men in same-sex marriages had many sexual partners outside of their marriages. The study revealed that homosexuals engaging in casual encounters had an average of 16-28 sexual partners each year, and those in so-called "steady" relationships had an average of 6-10 sex partners each year.[19]

These are just a few of the reasons many believe that the legalization of same-sex marriage will have a negative impact on traditional marriage. Once the government redefines marriage, many other kinds of marital relationships will be proposed and the sanctity of the marriage institution will be lost.

Does legalization of same-sex marriage really affect families?

Those who oppose same-sex marriage often point to the connection between marriage and family to support their arguments. Traditional marriages provide a moral and legal structure for children. Proponents of gay marriage point out that many married couples do not have children—thus the connection is irrelevant.

While it is true that some married couples do not have children due to choice or infertility, that does not invalidate the public purpose of marriage. Marriage is a public institution that brings together a father and mother to bring children into the world. Individuals may have all sorts of private reasons for marrying, but there is an established public purpose for marriage.

The fact some couples choose not to have children or are not able to have children does not invalidate this public purpose. We must be careful to note the distinction between *purpose* and *use*. For example, you are reading a book I have written. I would like to believe that every person who has a copy of one of my books has read it. But I know that is not true. Some of the books I've written sit on shelves, and others sit in boxes. Others sit in used bookstores. The fact that some people don't read my books doesn't mean the books were not intended to be read.

Likewise, we shouldn't assume that the connection between marriage and family is insignificant simply because some couples do not or cannot have children. One of the public purposes of traditional marriage is procreation.

At the center of every civilization is the family unit. There may be other social and political structures, but civilizations survive when the family survives, and they fall apart when the family falls apart. Michael Novak, a former professor and winner of the Templeton Prize for Progress in Religion, put it this way: "One unforgettable law has been learned through all the oppressions, disasters, and injustices of the last thousand years: if things go well with the family, life is worth living; when the family falters, life falls apart."[20]

It is marriages between a man and a woman who produce children that allows a civilization to exist and persist. A marriage is the foundation of a family, and families are the foundation of a civilization.

THE SOCIAL IMPACT OF HOMOSEXUALITY

THE HOMOSEXUAL AGENDA IS being promoted in the schools, in the corporate world, in entertainment, and in society at large. Christians are rightly concerned about the goals of the agenda and the recent rise in legal activism. Without question, there is a growing opposition to the biblical perspective on homosexuality.

For example, some activists are attempting to get legislative bodies to pass laws that would criminalize any actions Christians take based upon biblical injunctions regarding homosexuality. Liberal judges are handing down rulings that limit Christian teaching and witness concerning homosexuality. Other legal and political battles relate to such issues as hate crimes legislation and whether homosexuals can serve in the military. These issues need clear and concise discussion and resolution.

What are some signs of the growing opposition to the biblical perspective on homosexuality?

Often we can see the future in America by watching what has been taking place in Europe and Canada. In Sweden, pastor

Ake Green was sentenced to jail time for violating the Swedish hate-crime laws when he preached to his congregation on the subject of homosexuality. Ultimately the case was appealed to the highest court. Although Green was finally acquitted, he and other pastors will likely refrain from preaching on this topic anytime in the future.[1]

In Canada, public statements against homosexuality can be considered "inciting hatred" toward homosexuals. Such statements are considered illegal according to Canadian law, even if they are made from the pulpit. What constitutes "inciting hatred" is still unclear.[2]

A Canadian court also fined a man for submitting a newspaper advertisement in response to a homosexual pride week celebration. The ad included citations of four Bible verses that address homosexuality—Romans 1, Leviticus 18:22, Leviticus 20:13, and 1 Corinthians 6:9-10. But the man did not put the actual verses in the ad.[3]

John DeCicco is a city councillor in Kamloops, British Columbia. He was forced to apologize and pay a fine of $1000 to a homosexual activist simply because he said that homosexuality is "not normal and not natural."[4] The councillor said this because he is an active Catholic and a member of the Knights of Columbus and believes that homosexuality is counter to the teaching of the church. He is also an Italian immigrant who came to Canada when he was 15 and is fiercely proud of the country he now calls home.

Many wonder if it is really the councillor who was the victim in this situation and another earlier incident. Six months before, the councillor opposed a homosexual pride proclamation. Shortly thereafter his barbershop was vandalized and the words "Homophobia Die" were scrawled on the door of his business.

At the time he said, "I'm not against lesbian and gay people, but I don't agree that I should have to endorse it." He went on to say that people can do what they like in the privacy of their own homes, but they shouldn't "go out and flaunt it in front of people who don't necessarily agree."

The councillor apologized for his comments even though he was the one who was victimized by vandals. He was fined and forced to issue a statement saying his comments were "inappropriate and hurtful to some." He made the comments in a council meeting and in media interviews. He said he was not going to change his stand, but would be more careful about what he said in public.

Also, the Canadian Broadcast Standards Council rules have been used to censure radio programs that deal with the subject of homosexuality. In 1997, for example, the council ruled that the airing of a Focus on the Family program with Dr. James Dobson, called "Homosexuality: Fact and Fiction," violated their broadcast requirements.[5]

What about opposition in the United States?

Yes, similar examples of opposition can be found in the United States. In 2000, a Colorado woman became a Christian and withdrew from a lesbian relationship. When she and her former lesbian partner went to court over custody of her daughter, the court ordered her to "make sure that there is nothing in the religious upbringing or teaching that the minor child is exposed to that can be considered homophobic."[6]

In a Washington, DC court, a judge heard a case concerning a gay man who was refused communion in the Catholic Church because of his open homosexuality. The judge stated in her ruling to the man that "terrible violence was done to you when the body of Christ was denied to you. I am terribly sorry for what happened to you. As a member of the Church, I ask you to forgive our Church."[7]

Back in 1989, just as the late Cardinal John O'Connor was beginning his sermon in New York City's St. Patrick's Cathedral, members of the militant group ACT-UP began shouting. "You bigot, O'Connor, you're killing us," yelled one angry man. The group began stretching out in the aisles or chaining themselves to the pews. O'Connor attempted to continue the service. Police ended up arresting 43 protesters, including some who had to be carried out on stretchers because they refused to stand up. One protestor made his way to the altar for communion and took a wafer and threw it on the ground.[8]

On October 29, 2005, a mob of activists that some estimated at 1000 people left an antiwar demonstration and went to the Tremont Temple Baptist Church in Boston in order to disrupt a Love Won Out conference. This conference was one of many held around the country by Focus on the Family. It features former homosexuals and other speakers who explain how to overcome homosexual temptations.

The protest from the activists included a rash of shouted obscenities and some threats of violence. A truck with a loud-speaker parked near the front doors of the church, and someone shouted, "Shut it down! Shut it down!" Unfortunately, the city police took no action to disperse the crowd even though the mob had no permit to demonstrate in front of the church.[9]

Consider that Massachusetts law prohibits anyone from interfering with someone's constitutional right to freedom of speech. Thus, the people in the Love Won Out conference were within their legal rights. Still, the police took little action. They merely stood in front of the doors of the church, barring anyone from entering or leaving.

The protest did not happen spontaneously. Earlier that month, a gay activist Web site known as Queer Today called on homosexuals to protest the event. The posting said, "Queerphobia: Shut It Down. War: Shut It Down."

On October 10, 2004, six men and five women with a group known as Repent America were arrested in Philadelphia while preaching and speaking during a public homosexual celebration known as OutFest. This taxpayer-funded event was organized by Philly Pride Presents, Inc.

The Christians (later known as the Philadelphia Eleven) walked into the gathering singing hymns and carrying signs encouraging homosexuals to repent. They were immediately confronted by a militant group of gay activists known as the Pink Angels. These activists blew loud whistles and carried large pink signs in front of the Christians in order to block their message and access to the event. Many of the gay activists screamed obscenities at the Christians.

The Philadelphia police (apparently under the direction of Chief Inspector James Tiano, who was the city's "police liaison to the gay and lesbian community") refused to take any action as the Christians were continuously followed, obstructed, and harassed. A video posted on the Repent America Web site clearly showed that the Christians were respectfully cooperating with the police and obeying orders to move. Nevertheless, 11 Christians were arrested, but none of the Pink Angels were arrested.

Those arrested ranged in age from a 17-year-old girl to a 72-year-old grandmother. After the Christians spent 21 hours in jail, the Philadelphia district attorney's office charged five of them with various felonies and misdemeanors stemming from Pennsylvania's hate-crimes law. If the Philadelphia Eleven were convicted of these charges, they would have faced 47 years in prison and $90,000 in fines each.

Even though a video clearly showed that no criminal activity took place, the prosecution refused to withdraw the charges, and, in court, characterized the group's views as "hate speech." The judge for the Philadelphia County Court of Common Pleas finally dismissed the charges, saying that she found no basis whatsoever for any of them.[10]

The Philadelphia Eleven filed a federal lawsuit against the city of Philadelphia and Philly Pride Presents, Inc. for violations of their civil rights. But a judge ruled in that case that the police were permitted to discriminate against the plaintiffs because of safety concerns. Even though the judge conceded that "the activity in question took place in a public forum," and that "there is no doubt that the venue for OutFest, a designated section of streets and sidewalks of Philadelphia, was a public place," he concluded that "once the city issued a permit to Philly Pride for OutFest, it was empowered to enforce the permit by excluding persons expressing contrary messages."[11]

By contrast, when Repent America was the target of what many might call a "hate crime," no action was taken against the perpetrators. Less than a year later, a militant homosexual mob threatened the Christians with physical violence at Philadelphia's Gay Pride parade. This was a city-funded event that included simulated sex acts on some of the floats. Yet the police ignored the mistreatment of these Christians and even ignored the obscene displays in the parade and around it.

During the event, the Repent America members were "surrounded, obstructed and continuously harassed" by homosexual activists, many of whom wore handkerchief masks to hide their identities. It was later discovered that a group had earlier put out a news release before the parade, calling on supporters to stop the Christian group. The gay activists were told to gather near the "Queers Bash Back" and "No Human Liberation without Queer Liberation" banners.[12]

Should we pass hate crimes legislation?

Over the last few decades, there has been a major push for hate crimes legislation. The passage of such legislation has often been used to promote the homosexual agenda. Including sexual orientation as part of the hate crimes criminal code essentially equates gay rights with civil rights.

Even if we ignore the way gay activists have used hate-crimes legislation to promote their agenda, there are good reasons to reject such legislation. Years ago the American criminal justice system headed down the wrong road by enacting hate-crime bills. It turned the concept of equal protection under the law on its head by increasing the penalties for some crimes based on the race or sexual orientation of the victim.

Many commentators (of different ethnic and religious backgrounds) have pointed out that we don't need more criminal laws. We merely need to enforce the laws that already exist on the books. And that is true; someone has said that essentially we have 50,000 laws in America in order to enforce the Ten Commandments.

A major flaw with hate-crime laws is that they divide victims into two categories.

While they provide special protection for minorities, they provide no similar protection for the general population. *Every* member of society deserves equal protection, not just some groups and not others.

A second flaw in hate-crime laws is the flawed assumption that enhanced penalties help to deter crimes. There is scant evidence for this. Most hate crimes are "crimes of passion" and are not likely to be discouraged by greater criminal penalties. It is also very interesting that the argument for greater deterrence usually comes from those who argue that the death penalty has no deterrent effect. Do these advocates really believe that a hate-crime law will deter a criminal simply because he or she might spend a few extra months in jail?

Proponents of hate-crime laws argue that these laws are needed to protect ethnic minorities and people of different sexual orientation. But these laws are unnecessary. Criminal acts are *already* illegal. Adding additional penalties do not deter these crimes. Instead, they violate the constitutional right to equal protection for everyone. And they create a category in the law that essentially introduces the concept of a "thought crime."

Most totalitarian countries use some sort of "thought crime" laws that criminalize people's thoughts and intents. But now Western nations that have had long traditions of freedom (such as the United States, Canada, New Zealand, the United Kingdom, and Sweden) are experiencing challenges to these basic constitutional freedoms. In the end, hate-crime laws have become part of a key systematic strategy by gay activists to use sexual-orientation hate-crime laws to suppress dissent and criminalize biblical morality.

Point of View: It seems that the church has taken a politically correct approach by not addressing homosexuality as sin. Have we softened on some of these issues?

Dr. Timothy Dailey: I think this is one of the great dangers of the full acceptance of the homosexual lifestyle. With hate-crime legislation and legislation that grants domestic partners benefits…we are going to see…textbooks in our children's schools [that] aren't going to have pictures of a husband and a wife but instead will have pictures of two men with a family or two women with a family. This is already being mandated in California.

—Interview with **Dr. Timothy Dailey**
on *Point of View* radio talk[13]

Hate-crime laws criminalize *thought* rather than *conduct*. They punish people on account of their point of view. Criminal prosecutions delve into more than the defendant's intent; they inquire into the opinions about his or her victim. And trying to distinguish between opinions and prejudice is often difficult.

Former U.S. Supreme Court justice Oliver Wendell Holmes said, "If there is any principle of the Constitution that more imperatively calls for attachment than any other, it is the principle of free thought—not free thought for those who agree with us but freedom for the thought that we hate."[14]

We may not like what some people think, but we should not have laws on the books to punish them for their opinions. We already have laws on the books to punish people for improper conduct. Those laws are sufficient to punish those who commit crimes of hate.

What about gays in the military?

The current policy concerning homosexuals in the U.S. military is known as "Don't ask, don't tell." The policy prohibits anyone who engages in homosexual behavior from serving in the military. But the policy also requires that as long as gay or bisexual men or women hide their sexual orientation, their military superiors may not investigate their sexuality.

This compromise policy makes a distinction between homosexual orientation and homosexual conduct. Consider this quote from the Pentagon's policy guidelines on homosexuals in the military:

> Sexual orientation will not be a bar to service unless manifested by homosexual conduct. The military will discharge members who engage in homosexual conduct, which is defined as a homosexual act, a statement that the member is homosexual or bisexual, or a marriage or attempted marriage to someone of the same gender.[15]

When this policy was considered in 1993, there was controversy. Former Senator Barry Goldwater said in a letter to *The Washington Post* that the military should lift its ban on homosexuals. "You don't need to be 'straight' to fight and die for your country," he said. "You just need to shoot straight."[16]

Since 1993, when this policy was established by then-President Bill Clinton, there has been growing pressure to change it. Many other countries around the world allow homosexuals to serve in their military. The Amsterdam Treaty, for example, grants the European Union the power to combat discrimination based on sex, race or ethnic origin, religion, belief, disability, age, or sexual orientation.

Twelve former service members initiated a lawsuit against the "Don't ask, don't tell" policy following the Supreme Court's 2003 ruling in *Lawrence v. Texas.* They argued that because the high court had outlawed state antisodomy laws, there also needed to be a change in U.S. military policy.[17]

Gay rights groups also were encouraged that the European Court of Human Rights (Strasbourg, France) upheld gay rights in Ireland and ordered Britain to repeal all restrictions on homosexuals in the military. They felt this ruling strengthened their case because Justice Anthony Kennedy quoted from that court in the *Lawrence* decision.

Members of Congress have tried to change the policy through various legislative acts (including the Military Readiness Enhancement Act). In early 2007, the former chairman of the Joint Chiefs of Staff, General John Shalikashvili, wrote in an editorial that he believed it was time for the 1993 policy to be replaced with a military policy of nondiscrimination toward those of homosexual orientation.[18] He said that when he was chairman, there was concern among many in the military that homosexuality was incompatible with military service. There were concerns that accepting homosexual individuals would lower morale, harm recruitment efforts, and undermine unit cohesion. He believes that the public's and the military's views have since changed.

A poll done by *The Boston Globe* found that 79 percent of the general public found nothing wrong with openly gay people serving in the military.[19] Even more significant was a Zogby poll of those serving in the military, which showed that nearly three in four troops (73 percent) said they were personally comfortable in the presence of gays and lesbians in their midst.[20]

The current law makes it very clear that "there is no constitutional right to serve in the armed forces," and noted that living conditions in military quarters are often "spartan, primitive, and characterized by forced intimacy with little or no privacy."[21] Therefore, members of the armed services should not be forced to expose themselves to people who might be sexually attracted to them. And current laws also state that military standards of conduct apply at all times—both on-duty and off-duty.

Military life is fundamentally different from civilian life. In the military, individual liberty is subordinate to the mission. If someone is not able to meet certain qualifications for service, he or she is not selected for service and can be removed from his or her post. Those with backgrounds that indicate alcohol or drug abuse are not selected. Even if someone has a history of speeding tickets he or she may not be selected.

General Norman Schwarzkopf stated, "Whether we like it or not, in my years of military service, I have experienced the fact that the introduction of an open homosexual into a small unit immediately polarizes that unit and destroys the very bonding that is so important for the unit's survival in time of war."[22] General Colin Powell testified that open homosexuality in military units "involves matters of privacy and human sexuality that, in our judgment, if allowed to exist openly in the military, would affect the cohesion and well-being of the force."[23]

Are we as a society "defining deviancy down"?

More than a decade ago, Senator Daniel Patrick Moynihan wrote an important essay that has been quoted frequently through the years. He used the phrase "defining deviancy down" to describe the way antisocial, criminal behavior is being increasingly tolerated and explained away.[24]

When societies begin to show high levels of deviancy, they tend to define deviancy downward so they can live with their social circumstances. Otherwise, it becomes too uncomfortable to live in such a society. A perfect example is how, years ago, the American Psychiatric Society and society at large decided to redefine homosexuality.

A few years ago, Senator Sam Brownback borrowed from Moynihan's concept when he wrote a column entitled "Defining Marriage Down." He argued that marriage is at the center of the family and that redefining marriage would have devastating consequences. Over the last few decades, a social experiment has been taking place in Europe concerning marriage. In Europe, marriage has been redefined to include same-sex marriages, and this, in turn, has

> "As many advocates are putting it, 'What difference does it make to the government or an employer whom you are having sex with?' This sort of reductionism—a spouse is nothing more than a sex partner, so a sex partner is the same as a spouse—misses the point of what marriage is...So far, governments are resisting same-sex marriages. But instead, marriage is being defined down."[25]
>
> —**Gene Edward Veith**,
> Culture Editor of *World* magazine

changed society's perspective on marriage and ended up weakening marriage as an institution.[26]

Not only has society been willing to define deviancy down, it has also been willing to define deviancy up. Charles Krauthammer wrote a column that gives examples of things that used to be considered normal but are now called deviant. He believes that there is "a complimentary social phenomenon that goes with defining deviancy down. As part of the vast social project of moral leveling, it is not enough for the deviant to be normalized. The normal must be found to be deviant." In the context of this discussion, those who make moral judgments about homosexuality are deviant. He explained it in this way:

> One way is denial: Defining real deviancy down creates the pretense that deviance has disappeared because it is been redefined as normal. Another strategy is distraction: Defining deviancy up creates brand new deviancies that we can now go off and fight. That distracts us from the old deviancy and gives us the feeling that, despite the murder and mayhem and madness around us, we are really preserving and policing our norms.[27]

So that which is deviant is redefined as normal, and that which is normal is declared deviant. Or, as Isaiah 5:20 puts it, "Woe to those who call evil good, and good evil; who substitute darkness for light and light for darkness; who substitute bitter for sweet, and sweet for bitter!" Essentially the values of our society have been inverted so that we are willing to call evil good, and good evil.

A FINAL WORD

THROUGHOUT THIS BOOK I have attempted to keep two biblical principles in tension. On the one hand we as Christians must stay true to our biblical convictions, and on the other hand, we should reach out with biblical compassion. This is what it means to speak the truth in love (Ephesians 4:15).

On the one hand, it is crucial for us to understand how the homosexual agenda threatens to redefine marriage and normalize homosexuality. Moreover, gay activists are pushing their agenda into the courts, the legislature, and the court of public opinion. Ultimately, this will threaten biblical authority and many of our personal and religious freedoms. Christians, therefore, must stand for truth.

On the other hand, it is also important for us to reach out to homosexuals and offer God's grace and redemption. We cannot let the hardened rhetoric of gay activists keep us from having Christ's heart toward homosexuals. As individuals and as the church, we should reach out to those caught in the sin of homosexuality and offer them hope and point them to Jesus Christ so that they will find freedom from the sexual sin that binds their lives.

I trust this book has been helpful in both ways. Also, let me encourage you to read some of the books that I have listed in the bibliography so that you can become even better prepared to stand for truth and express love in our culture.

Percentage of Voters in Support of State Marriage Amendments

State	Percentage of Voters (%)	Year
South Dakota	52	2006
Colorado	56	2006
Virginia	57	2006
Oregon	59	2004
Michigan	59	2004
Wisconsin	59	2006
Ohio	62	2004
Idaho	63	2006
Utah	66	2004
Nevada	67	2002
Montana	67	2004
Alaska	68	1998
Hawaii	69	1998
Nebraska	70	2000
Kansas	70	2005
Missouri	71	2004
North Dakota	73	2004
Arkansas	75	2004
Kentucky	75	2004
Georgia	76	2004
Texas	76	2005
Oklahoma	76	2004
Louisiana	78	2004
South Carolina	78	2006
Alabama	81	2006
Tennessee	81	2006
Mississippi	86	2004

BIBLIOGRAPHY

Alan Chambers, ed., *God's Grace and the Homosexual Next Door* (Eugene, OR: Harvest House, 2006).

Joe Dallas, *Desires in Conflict: Answering the Struggle for Sexual Identity* (Eugene, OR: Harvest House, 1991).

Joe Dallas, *The Gay Gospel: How Pro-Gay Advocates Misread the Bible* (Eugene, OR: Harvest House, 2007).

Joe Dallas, *When Homosexuality Hits Home* (Eugene, OR: Harvest House, 2004).

Bob Davies and Anita Worthen, *Someone I Love Is Gay* (Downers Grove, IL: InterVarsity Press, 1996).

Mike Haley, *101 Frequently Asked Questions about Homosexuality* (Eugene, OR: Harvest House, 2004).

D. James Kennedy and Jerry Newcombe, *What's Wrong with Same-sex Marriage?* (Wheaton, IL: Crossway Books, 2004).

Erwin Lutzer, *The Truth About Same-sex Marriage* (Chicago: Moody Publishers, 2004).

Joseph Nicolosi and Linda Ames Nicolosi, *A Parent's Guide to Preventing Homosexuality* (Downers Grove, IL: InterVarsity Press, 2002).

Alan Sears and Craig Osten, *The Homosexual Agenda* (Nashville, TN: Broadman and Holman, 2003).

Glenn T. Stanton and Dr. Bill Maier, *Marriage on Trial: The Case Against Same-sex Marriage and Parenting* (Downers Grove, IL: InterVarsity Press, 2004).

NOTES

Chapter 1—Homosexuality and Society

1. Marshall Kirk and Hunter Madsen, *After the Ball* (New York: Penguin Books, 1989).

2. Ibid.

3. Marshall Kirk and Erastes Pill, "The overhauling of straight America," *Guide,* November 1987.

4. Ibid.

5. Ibid.

6. Ibid.

7. Ibid.

8. Human Rights Campaign Web site, http://www.hrc.org/Template cfm?Section= About_HRC.

9. GLAAD Web site, http://www.glaad.org/about/mission.php.

10. NGLTF Web site, http://www.thetaskforce.org/about_us/mission_statements.

11. Lambda Legal Defense Web site, http://www.lambdalegal.org/cgi-bin/iowa/ about/index.html.

12. Jeffrey Satinover, *Homosexuality and the Politics of Truth* (Grand Rapids, MI: Baker Books, 1996), 33.

13. Dr. Charles Socarides, *Homosexuality: A Freedom Too Far* (Phoenix, AZ: Adam Margrave Books, 1995), 74.

14. "Dr. Charles Silverstein: An update on his professional contributions," *NARTH Bulletin,* March 1994, 5.

15. "U.S. psychiatrists' view on homosexuality differs from colleagues in foreign countries," *NARTH Bulletin,* November 1993, 6.

16. Brian McNaught, *Gay Issues in the Workplace* (New York: St. Martin's Press, 1993), 10.

Chapter 2—Homosexuality and Relationships

1. Felicity Barringer, "Sex survey of American men finds 1% are gay," *New York Times,* April 15, 1993, 1A.

2. Alfred Kinsey et al., *Sexual Behavior in the Human Male* (Philadelphia, PA: W.B. Saunders, 1948), 650-51.

3. Judith Reisman and Edward Eichel, *Kinsey, Sex and Fraud* (Lafayette, LA: Huntington House, 1990), 22.

4. Ibid., 29.

5. Marshall Kirk and Hunter Madsen, *After the Ball* (New York: Doubleday, 1989), 47.

6. T.C. Quinn et al., *New England Journal of Medicine,* September 8, 1983, 576-82.

7. Alan Bell and Martin Weinberg, *Homosexualities, a Study of Diversity Among Men and Women* (New York: Simon and Schuster, 1978), 308.

8. Alan Bell, Martin Weinberg, and S.K. Hammersmith, *Sexual Preference: Its Development in Men and Women* (Bloomington, IN: Indiana University Press, 1981), 308.

9. Maria Xiridou et al., "The contribution of steady and casual partnerships to the incidence of HIV infection among homosexual men in Amsterdam," *AIDS,* May 2, 2003, 1029-38.

10. Andrew Sullivan, *Virtually Normal* (New York: Vintage, 1996), 202-03.

11. Paul Gibson, "Gay Male and Lesbian Youth Suicide," originally in the "Report of the Secretary's Task Force on Youth Suicide," January 1989.

12. Dr. Louis W. Sullivan, M.D., Secretary of Health and Human Services, letter to Representative William E. Dannemeyer, October 1989.

13. F. Parris, "Some die young," *Washington Blade,* May 17, 1985.

14. Ritch Savin-Williams, "Suicide attempts among sexual minority youths: Population and measurement issues," *Journal of Consulting and Clinical Psychology,* (2001), 983-91.

15. Peter LaBarbara, "The gay youth suicide myth," *The Journal of Human Sexuality* (Carrolton, TX: Lewis and Stanley, 1996), 65-72.

16. N.E. Reiner, F.N. Judson, W.W. Bond, D.P. Francis, and N.J. Peterson, "Asymptomatic rectal mucosal lesions and hepatitis B surface antigen at sites of sexual contact in homosexual men with persistent hepatitis B virus infection," *Annals of Internal Medicine,* 1984, 170-73.

17. *HIV/AIDS Surveillance Report* (Atlanta, GA: Centers for Disease Control and Prevention, 1993), 13.

18. Catherine Hutchison et al., "Characteristics of patients with syphilis attending Baltimore STD clinics, *Archives of Internal Medicine,* 1991, 513.

19. "AMA profiles of adolescent health series," *America's Adolescents: How Healthy Are They?* (Chicago: The American Medical Association, 1990), 31.

20. A. Edwards and R.N. Thin, "Sexually transmitted diseases in lesbians," *Internal Journal of STD/AIDS,* May 1990 and C.J. Skinner et al., "A case-controlled study of sexual health needs of lesbians," *Genitourin Medical,* August 1996, 227.

21. R.S. Hoog, S.A. Strathdee et al., "Modeling the impact of HIV disease on mortality in gay and bisexual men," *International Journal of Epidemiology,* 1997, 659.

Chapter 3—Homosexuality and Families

1. Linda Waite and Maggie Gallagher, *The Case for Marriage: Why Married People Are Happier, Healthier, and Better off Financially* (New York: Doubleday, 2000).

2. Linda J. Waite, *The Ties that Bind: Perspectives on Marriage and Cohabitation* (New York: Aldine de Gruyter, 2000), 368-91.

3. Scott Christopher, "Sexuality in marriage, dating, and other relationships: A decade review," *Journal of Marriage and Family,* November 2000, 999-1017.

4. Peggy McDonough, "Chronic stress and the social patterning of women's health in Canada," *Social Science and Medicine,* 2002, 767-82.

5. Allan Horwitz, "Becoming married and mental health: A longitudinal study of a cohort of young adults," *Journal of Marriage and the Family,* November 1996, 895-907.

6. Paul Strand, "Cause and effect: The benefits of traditional marriage," http://www.cbn.com/CBNNews/News/040510a.aspx.

7. Patrick Fagan et al., "The positive effects of marriage: Economic effects of marriage," The Heritage Foundation, http://www.heritage.org/Research/Features?Marriage/economic.cfm.

8. Patrick Fagan et al., "The positive effects of marriage: Economic effects of marriage on welfare," The Heritage Foundation, http://www.heritage.org/Research/Features?Marriage/welfare.cfm.

9. Patrick Fagan et al., "The positive effects of marriage: Economic effects of marriage on adults," The Heritage Foundation, http://www.heritage.org/Research/Features?Marriage/adults.cfm.

10. Patrick Fagan et al., "The positive effects of marriage: Economic effects of marriage on children," The Heritage Foundation, http://www.heritage.org/Research/Features?Marriage/children.cfm.

11. See the U.S. Department of Labor Web site for the various longitudinal studies, http://www.bls.gov/nls/home.htm.

12. James Dobson, *Marriage Under Fire* (Sisters, OR: Multnomah, 2004), 54.

13. See J.D. Unwin, *Sexual Regulations and Human Behavior* (London: Williams & Norgate, 1933).

14. Michael Craven, *The Death of Marriage?* Center for Christ and Culture, October 23, 2006, http://www.battlefortruth.org/ArticlesDetail.asp?id=212&rr=1.

15. Robert Gebeloff and Mary Jo Patterson, "Married and gay couples are not all that different," *Times-Picayune,* November 22, 2003.

16. Timothy J. Dailey, "Comparing the lifestyles of homosexual couples to married couples," *Family Research Council Insight, http://www.frc.org/get.cfm?i=IS04C02.*

17. Matthew Bramlett and William Mosher, "First marriage dissolution, divorce and remarriage: United States," *National Center for Health Statistics,* May 31, 2001, 1.

18. "Largest gay study examines 2004 relationships," *GayWire Latest Breaking Releases,* www.glcensus.org.

19. Maria Xiridou, et al., "The contribution of steady and casual partnership to the incidence of HIV infection among homosexual men in Amsterdam," *AIDS,* 2003, 1031.

20. M. Pollack, "Male Homosexuality," in *Western Sexuality: Practice and Precept in Past and Present Times* (New York: Blackwell, 1985), 40-61.

21. Michael Wiederman, "Extramarital sex: prevalence and correlates in a national survey," *Journal of Sex Research,* 1997, 170.

22. E.O. Laumann et al., *The Social Organization of Sexuality: Sexual Practices in the United States* (Chicago: University of Chicago Press, 1994), 216.

23. A.P. Bell and M.S. Weinberg, *Homosexualities: A Study of Diversity Among Men and Women* (New York: Simon and Schuster, 1978), 308-09.

24. Maria Xiridou, "The contribution of steady and casual partnership," 1031.

25. David McWhirter and Andrew Mattison, *The Male Couple: How Relationships Develop* (Englewood Cliffs, NJ: Prentice-Hall, 1984), 252-53.

26. Interview from "Answering the Gay Deception," Renewing America's Mind DVD (Dallas: Point of View, 2006).

27. Timothy J. Dailey, "Comparing the lifestyles of homosexual couples."

28. Gary Remafedi et al., "Demography of sexual orientation in adolescents," *Pediatrics,* April 1992, 714-21, http://pediatrics.aappublications.org/cgi/content/abstract/89/4/714.

29. "Homosexuality and Teens: An Interview with Dr. Jeffrey Satinover," Massachusetts Family Institute, March 2003, http://www.mafamily.org/Marriage%20He aring%202003/satinover2.htm.

30. Ellen C. Perrin, "Technical Report: Coparent and second-parent adoption by same-sex parents," *Pediatrics,* 2002, 341.

31. Kristin Anderson Moore et al., "Marriage from a child's perspective: How does family structure affect children and what can we do about it?" *Child Trends Research Brief,* June 2002, 1.

32. Mary Parke, "Are married parents really better for children?" *Center for Law and Social Policy,* May 2003, 1.

33. Glenn T. Stanton and Bill Maier, *Marriage on Trial* (Downers Grove, IL: Inter-Varsity, 2004), 80.

34. M.A. Gold, Ellen Perrin et al., "Children of gay or lesbian parents," *Pediatrics in Review,* 1994, 354-58.

35. David Demo and Martha Cox, "Families with young children: A review of research in the 1990s," *Journal of Marriage and the Family,* 2000, 889.

Chapter 4—Homosexuality and the Schools

1. For more information see Sue Bohlin, "Helping teens understand homosexuality," at http://www.probe.org/faith-and-sexuality/homosexuality/ helping-teens-understand-homosexuality.html.

2. Peter Freiberg, "Study: Alcohol use more prevalent for lesbians," *The Washington Blade,* January 12, 2001, 21. Karen Paige Erickson, and Karen F. Trocki, "Sex, alcohol and sexually transmitted diseases: A national survey," *Family Planning Perspectives,* December 1994, 261.

3. Many such testimonies can be found at the Exodus International Web site at http://exodus.to, and the Stonewall Revisited Web site at http://stonewall revisited.com.

4. "'Governor's commission for gay youth' retreats to 'safety' and 'suicide,'" *The Massachusetts News,* December 2000.

5. Robert Garofalo et al., "The association between health risk behaviors and sexual orientation among a school-based sample of adolescents," *Pediatrics,* May 1998, 895-902.

6. Debra Saunders, "Gay-ed for tots," *Weekly Standard,* August 19, 1996, 21.

7. GLSEN Web site, www.glsen.org.

8. Linda Harvey, "Children at risk: GLSEN, corruption and crime," Mission America, 2003, http://www.missionamerica.com/oldagenda26.php.

9. PFLAG Web site, www.pflag.org.

10. Linda Harvey, "The world according to PFLAG," Mission America, 2003, http://www.missionamerica.com/stoppflag2.php.

11. Marilyn Elias, "Gay teens coming out earlier to peers and family," *USA Today*, February 8, 2007, 1A.

12. Linda Harvey, "Homosexual clubs: The rest of the story," Mission America, 2003, http://www.missionamerica.com/agenda.php?articlenum=35.

13. "The legal liability associated with homosexual education in public schools," Citizens for Community Values, http://www.ccv.org/Legal_Liability_of_Homosexuality_Education.htm.

14. Ibid.

15. R.S. Hogg et al., "Modeling the impact of HIV disease on mortality in gay and bisexual men," *International Journal of Epidemiology*, 1997, 657-61.

16. "Health implications associated with homosexuality," monograph published by The Medical Institute for Sexual Health, 1999.

17. Robert Garofalo, *Pediatrics*, 1998.

18. Theo G.M. Sandfort et al., "Same-sex sexual behavior and psychiatric disorders," *Archives of General Psychiatry*, January 2001, 85-91.

19. "The dirty dozen: America's most bizarre and politically correct college courses," *YAF*, December 19, 2006, http://media.yaf.org/latest/12_19_06.cfm.

20. "D'oh! More know Simpsons than Constitution," MSNBC, March 1, 2006, http://www.msnbc.msn.com/id/11611015.

21. Lois Romano, "Literacy of college graduates is in decline," *The Washington Post*, December 25, 2005, A12.

Chapter 5—Causes of Homosexuality

1. Sherwood Cole, "Biology, homosexuality, and moral culpability," *Bibliotheca Sacra*, July-September 1997, 355.

2. Simon LeVay, "A difference in hypothalamic structure between heterosexual and homosexual men," *Science*, August 30, 1991, 1034-37.

3. David Gelman, "Born or bred?" *Newsweek*, February 24, 1992, 46.

4. Michael Bailey and Richard Pillard, "A genetic study of male sexual orientation," *Archives of General Psychiatry*, 1991, 1089-96.

5. Joe Dallas, *Desire in Conflict* (Eugene, OR: Harvest House, 1991), 90.

6. Gelman, "Born or bred?" 46.

7. Gelman, "Born or bred?" 46.

8. Dean Hamer et al., "A linkage between DNA markers on the X chromosome and male sexual orientation," *Science,* July 16, 1993, 321-27.

9. "Study links homosexuality to genetics," *Dallas Morning News,* July 16, 1993, 1A.

10. Cole, "Biology, homosexuality, and moral culpability," 357.

11. Dallas, *Desires in Conflict,* 96.

12. Interview from "Answering the Gay Deception," Renewing America's Mind DVD (Dallas: Point of View, 2006).

13. Dallas, *Desires in Conflict,* 96.

14. John Money, *Gay, Straight, and In-Between* (Baltimore, MD: Johns Hopkins University Press, 1988), 117.

15. Glenn Wood and John Dietrich, *The AIDS Epidemic: Balancing Compassion and Justice* (Portland, OR: Multnomah, 1990), 238.

16. Ruben Fine, *Psychoanalytic Theory, Male and Female Homosexuality: Psychological Approaches* (New York: New York Center for Psychoanalytic Training, 1987), 84.

17. Michael Cavanaugh, *Make Your Tomorrow Better* (New York: Paulist Press, 1980), 266.

18. Charles Socarides, *Homosexuality: Psychoanalytic Therapy* (New York: Jason Aronson, Inc., 1979), 3.

19. Robert L. Switzer, "Can some gay men and lesbians change their sexual orientation?" *Archives of Sexual Behavior,* October 2003, 403-17.

20. Laura Sessions Stepp, "Partway gay? For some teen girls, sexual preference is a shifting concept," *The Washington Post,* January 4, 2004, D-1.

21. Lisa Diamond, "Was it a phase? Young women's relinquishment of lesbian/bisexual identities over a 5-year period." *Journal of Personality and Social Psychology,* 84, 352-64.

22. William Masters and Virginia Johnson, *Homosexuality in Perspective* (Boston: Little, Brown and Co., 1979), 402.

23. "Public opinion trends on gay marriage," The Pew Forum on Religion and Public Life, http://pewforum.org/docs/index.php?DocID=147.

24. Joseph Shapiro, "Straight talk about gays," *U.S. News & World Report,* July 15, 1993, 48.

Chapter 6—Homosexuality and the Bible

1. Two prominent prohomosexual commentators are Sherwin Bailey, *Homosexuality and the Western Christian Tradition* (London: Longmans, Green, 1955;

reprint, Hamden, CT: Shoestring Press, 1975), and John Boswell, *Christianity, Social Tolerance, and Homosexuality* (Chicago: University of Chicago Press, 1980).

2. Letha Scanzoni and Virginia Ramey Mollenkott, *Is the Homosexual My Neighbor?* (San Francisco: Harper & Row, 1978), 60-61.

3. Robert Gagnon, *The Bible and Homosexual Practice: Texts and Hermeneutics* (Nashville, TN: Abingdon Press, 2001), 229-30.

Chapter 7—Homosexuality and the Church

1. Stanton Jones and Mark Yarhouse, *Homosexuality: The Use of Scientific Research in the Church's Moral Debate* (Downers Grove, IL: InterVarsity Press, 2000), 149-50.

2. Stephen Bennett, "Was Jesus gay?" WorldNetDaily, July 16, 2002, http://www.wnd.com/news/article.asp?ARTICLE_ID=28290.

3. Ibid.

4. Randy Thomas, "Understanding the Three Degrees of Homosexuality," in *God's Grace and the Homosexual Next Door* (Eugene, OR: Harvest House, 2006), 120-30.

5. Ibid., 122.

6. Ibid., 126.

7. Mona Riley and Brad Sargent, *Unwanted Harvest* (Nashville, TN: Broadman & Holman Publishers, 1995), 60.

8. Sue Bohlin, "When someone in your congregation says 'I'm gay,'" Probe Ministries Web site, http://www.probe.org/faith-and-sexuality/homosexuality/when-someone-in-your-congregation-says-im-gay.html.

Chapter 8—Same-sex Marriage and Politics

1. *Baehr v. Lewin,* 852 P.2d 44 (Hawaii, 1993).

2. *Baehr v. Miike,* 910 P.2d 112 (Hawaii, 1996).

3. *Baker v. State,* 744 A.2d 864 (Vermont, 1999).

4. Defense of Marriage Act, § 1 U.S.C.A, § 7 (1996).

5. *Brause v. Bureau of Vital Statistics,* 1998 WL 88743 (Alaska Super., 1998).

6. Ira Glasser, ACLU executive director, "Civil Liberties at Risk through Ballot Initiatives," ACLU press release, November 4, 1998.

7. *Lawrence v. Texas,* 539 U.S. 558 (2003).

8. *Goodrich v. Department of Public Health,* 798 N.E.2d 941 (Massachusetts, 2003).

9. Opinions of the justices to the Senate, SJC 09163 (February 3, 2004).

10. Sam Brownback, "Defining marriage down," *National Review,* July 9, 2004, http://www.nationalreview.com/comment/brownback200407090921.asp.

11. Michael Foust, "Same-sex marriage: Coming to a state near you?" *BP News,* November 26, 2003, http://www.bpnews.net/bpnews.asp?ID=17172.

12. Foust, "Same-sex marriage."

13. Matt Foreman, executive director of National Gay and Lesbian Task Force, http://www.wusa9.com/printfullstory.aspx?storyid=34534.

14. Ibid.

15. Alan Cooperman, "Little consensus on marriage amendment," *The Washington Post,* February 14, 2004, A1.

16. "Talking about civil marriage equality," http://www.hrcactioncenter.org/action-center/talking.html.

17. Michael Foust, "Would religious freedoms be violated by same-sex 'marriage'?" *BP News,* March 12, 2004, http://www.bpnews.net/printerfriendly.asp?ID=17839.

18. Joel Belz, "A totally alien mindset," *World,* March 20, 2004, http://www.worldmag.com/articles/8642.

19. Mary Ann Glendon, "For better or for worse?" *Wall Street Journal,* February 25, 2004, http://www.opinionjournal.com/editorial/feature.html?id=110004735.

20. Paul Strand, "Cause and effect: The benefits of traditional marriage," http://www.cbn.com/CBNNews/News/040510a.aspx.

21. Jeff Jacoby, "Adoption, kids and the gay agenda," March 16, 2006, http://www.townhall.com/columnists/JeffJacoby/2006/03/16/adoption,_kids,_and_the_gay_agenda.

22. See www.smrb.com.

23. See www.glcensus.org.

24. Lou Chaibbaro, "Log Cabin questions need for ENDA, angering activists, GOP lawmakers," *Washington Blade,* May 13, 2002.

Chapter 9—Answering the Arguments for Same-sex Marriage

1. Greg Koukl, "Same-sex marriage challenges and responses," "Solid Ground," *Stand to Reason,* May 2004, http://www.str.org/site/News2?page=NewsArticle&id=6553.

2. Peter Sprigg, "Questions on same-sex unions answered," Family Research Council blog, http://www.frc.org/get.cfm?i=PV03J01&f=PG03I03.

3. Robert Spitzer, "Can some gay men and lesbians change their sexual orientation?" *Archives of Sexual Behavior,* (2003), 403-17.

4. J.C. Gutin, "End of the rainbow," *Discover,* November 1994, 71-75.

5. *Loving v. Virginia,* U.S. Supreme Court, 388 U.S. 1, 1967.

6. *Baker v. Nelson,* Supreme Court of Minnesota, 1971.

7. Michaelangelo Signorile, "I do, I do, I do, I do, I do," *OUT,* May 1996, 30-32.

8. Jeff Jacoby, "Gay marriage would change society's ideal," *Boston Globe,* July 6, 2003, H11.

9. Ibid.

10. Stanley Kurtz, "The end of marriage in Scandinavia: The conservative case for same-sex marriage collapses," *The Weekly Standard,* February 2, 2004, http://www.weeklystandard.com/Content/Public/Articles/000/000/003/660zypwj.asp.

11. Stanley Kurtz, "Dutch debate: Despite a challenge, the evidence stands: Marriage is in decline in the Netherlands," *National Review,* July 21, 2004, http://www.nationalreview.com/kurtz/kurtz200407210936.asp.

12. Alexandria Sage, "Utah polygamy ban is challenged: U.S. Supreme Court's sodomy ruling is cited," *Associated Press,* January 26, 2004.

13. "The Supreme Court: Excerpts from Supreme Court's decision striking down sodomy laws," *New York Times,* June 27, 2003, A18.

14. Judith Levine, "Stop the wedding: Why gay marriage isn't radical enough," *Village Voice,* July 29, 2003, 40.

15. Stanley Kurtz, "Beyond gay marriage," *Weekly Standard,* August 4, 2003.

16. Michael Kinsley, "Abolish marriage: Let's really get the government out of our bedrooms," *The Washington Post,* July 3, 2004, A23.

17. Justin Katz, "One man's marriage trap: The ever-shifting, deeply conflicted Andrew Sullivan," *National Review,* December 31, 2004, http://www.national-review.com/issue/katz200501070843.asp.

18. Em and Lo, "The new monogamy," *New York,* November 21, 2005, http://nymag.com/lifestyle/sex/annual/2005/15063/index.html.

19. Maria Xiridou et al., "The contribution of steady and casual partnerships to the incidence of HIV infection among homosexual men in Amsterdam," *AIDS,* May 2, 2003, 1029-38.

20. Michael Novak, "The family out of favor," *Harper's Magazine,* April 1976, 37-46.

Chapter 10—The Social Impact of Homosexuality

1. "Swedish pastor acquitted of hate speech charges, *WorldNetDaily*, November 29, 2005, http://www.worldnetdaily.com/news/article.asp?ARTICLE_ID=47633.

2. Art Moore, "The Bible as hate literature," *WorldNetDaily*, October 21, 2002, http://www.worldnetdaily.com/news/article.asp?ARTICLE_ID=29328.

3. Art Moore, "Bible verses regarded as hate literature," *WorldNetDaily*, February 18, 2003, http://www.wnd.com/news/article.asp?ARTICLE_ID=31080.

4. John-Henry Westen and Gudrun Schultz, "Canadian city councillor fined $1000 for saying homosexuality 'not normal or natural,'" LifeSiteNews.com, January 19, 2007, http://www.lifesite.net/ldn/2007/jan/07011902.html.

5. Art Moore, "The Bible as hate literature."

6. Valerie Richardson, "Mother appeals ruling on gays," *The Washington Times*, November 5, 2003, http://www.washtimes.com/national/20031105-122726-4541r.htm.

7. Kara Speltz, "A homily in three parts: Encountering grace in the courtroom," Whosever: An Online Magazine for Gay, Lesbian, Bisexual and Transgender Christians, March/April 2003, http://www.whosoever.org/v7i5/kara.shtml.

8. Ed Magnuson, "In a rage over AIDS: A militant protest group targets the Catholic Church," *Time*, September 25, 1989.

9. "Homosexual activists terrorize Boston church during ex-gay conference while people watch," http://www.article8.org/docs/news_events/love_won_out/conf_1029.htm.

10. "Judge drops all charges against Philly Christians," WorldNetDaily, February 17, 2005, http://www.worldnetdaily.com/news/article.asp?ARTICLE_ID=42905.

11. "Federal court rules against Philly eleven in civil case," January 23, 2007, Americans for Truth Web site, http://americansfortruth.com/issues/the-agenda-glbtq-activist-groups/state-glbtq-activist-groups/philly-pride/.

12. "Gay pride features simulated sex, attacking mob," WorldNetDaily, June 14, 2005, http://www.worldnetdaily.com/news/article.asp?ARTICLE_ID=44753.

13. Interview from "Answering the Gay Deception," Renewing America's Mind DVD (Dallas: Point of View, 2006).

14. Oliver Wendell Holmes, *United States v. Schwimmer* 279 U.S. 644 (1929).

15. "Gay rights in the military: The Pentagon's new policy guidelines on homosexuals in the military," *The New York Times*, July 20, 1993, A-16.

16. As cited in http://query.nytimes.com/gst/fullpage.html?res=9F0CE0D6173EF9 32A25755C0A965958260&n=Top%2fReference%2fTimes%20Topics%2fPeo ple%2fG%2fGoldwater%2c%20Barry%20M%2e.

17. "Efforts intensify to end gay soldier ban," Associated Press, June 14, 2005, http://sfgate.com/cgi-bin/article.cgi?f=/n/a/2005/06/14/national/a122329D46. DTL.

18. John H Shalikashvili, "Second thoughts on gays in the military," *The New York Times,* January 2, 2007, http://www.nytimes.com/2007/01/02/opinion/ 02shalikashvili.html?ex=1168491600&en=30819a730f9f96bd&ei=5070.

19. Scott S. Greenberger, "One year later, nation divided on gay marriage," *The Boston Globe,* May 15, 2005, http://www.boston.com/news/specials/gay_ marriage/articles/2005/05/15/one_year_later_nation_divided_on_gay_marriage/.

20. "Don't ask, don't tell not working: Survey indicates shift in military attitudes," Zogby Poll, December 18, 2006, http://www.zogby.com/NEWS/ReadNews .dbm?ID=1222.

21. Public Law 103-160, Section 654, Title 10.

22. Statement by General Norman Schwarzkopf at hearings on May 11, 1993, http://dont.stanford.edu/hearings/Hearings5-11-93.pdf.

23. Statement by General Colin Powell at hearings on July 20, 1993, http://dont .stanford.edu/hearings/Hearings7-20-93.pdf.

24. Daniel Patrick Moynihan, "Defining deviancy down" *The American Scholar,* Winter 1993, vol. 62, no. 1, 17-30.

25. Gene Edward Veith, "Wages for sin: Marriage benefits are starting to go to those who are shacking up," *World,* August 18, 2001, http://www.worldmag. com/articles/5309.

26. Sam Brownback, "Defining marriage down," *National Review,* July 9, 2004, http://www.nationalreview.com/comment/brownback200407090921.asp.

27. Charles Krauthammer, "Defining deviancy up," speech from September 13, 1993, http://www.aei.org/publications/pubID.17965,filter.all/pub_detail.asp.

More Excellent Harvest House Books on Homosexuality

When Homosexuality Hits Home
Joe Dallas

The heart–wrenching declaration that a loved one is a homosexual is increasingly being heard in Christian households across America. How can this be? What went wrong? Is there a cure?

Joe Dallas offers practical counsel, step by step, on how to deal with the many conflicts and emotions parents, grandparents, brothers and sisters or any family member will experience when learning of a loved one's homosexuality.

101 Frequently Asked Questions About Homosexuality
Mike Haley

Almost daily we hear reports that confirm the acceptance of homosexuality in our culture. Homosexuals are adopting children, appearing as characters on television programs, taking vacations catering to an exclusively gay clientele, and even seeking the right to "marry" their partners. But is this acceptance healthy for society? Here are the answers to the most often-asked questions about homosexuality, fielded by an expert on the subject and a former homosexual himself.

Restoring Sexual Identity
Anne Paulk

Is lesbianism inherited or is it developed in childhood? Does becoming a Christian eliminate sexual desire for members of the same sex? What support is available for women who struggle with lesbianism? Can a woman be a lesbian and a Christian at the same time? How does childhood sexual abuse relate to the development of lesbianism? These and other questions are answered as the author draws from her own experience and that of many other former lesbians.

God's Grace and the Homosexual Next Door
Alan Chambers and the Leadership Team at Exodus International

Author Alan Chambers—a former homosexual himself—and four of his colleagues at Exodus International offer practical and biblical insights on how both individuals and churches can become a haven for homosexuals seeking freedom from same–sex attraction. Winner of the *Outreach* Magazine Best Target Outreach Resource of 2007.